AF338277

The Name Israel

The Name Israel

MICHAEL J. ALTER

Foreword by Jeremy Barras

RESOURCE *Publications* · Eugene, Oregon

THE NAME ISRAEL

Resource Publications
An Imprint of Wipf and Stock Publishers
199 W. 8th Ave., Suite 3
Eugene, OR 97401

www.wipfandstock.com

PAPERBACK ISBN: 978-1-6667-6703-2
HARDCOVER ISBN: 978-1-6667-6704-9
EBOOK ISBN: 978-1-6667-6705-6

03/07/23

"Scripture quotations taken from the (NASB®) New American Standard Bible®, Copyright © 1960, 1971, 1977, 1995, 2020 by The Lockman Foundation. Used by permission. All rights reserved. www.lockman.org"

Credit: Rabbi Lord Jonathan Sacks, 'I Believe: A Weekly Reading of the Jewish Bible', on parshat Vayishlach, Koren Publishers, September 2022

Rabbi Yehoshua Alt. "The Fight For The 100 Brachos"
November 23, 2018 http://www.nevehzion.org/wp-content/uploads/2018/11/Vayishlach-2018-Rabbi-Alt. Used by permission from Rabbi Yehoshua Alt.

Rabbi Danny Burkeman. "The Pride of Our Name - Torah from around the world #92" World Union for Progressive Judaism April 23, 2017. Used by permission from Rabbi Danny Burkeman.

Rabbi Alex Israel. "Vayishlach Jacob, Esau and the Angel: "Shiur. SECTION III – 'The Transformation of Yaakov.'" Used by permission from Rabbi Alex Israel.

To
K'lal Ysrael

Genesis 12 *Now the Lord said to Abram,*

"Go from your country,

And from your relatives

And from your father's house,

To the land which I will show you;

2 And I will make you into a great nation,

And I will bless you,

And make your name great;

And you shall be a blessing;

3 And I will bless those who bless you,

And the one who curses you I will curse.

And in you all the families of the earth will be blessed."[1] (NASB)

---

1. The first command given to the father of the Children of Israel (the Jewish people) was to go to Israel, the Promised Land.

Contents

Foreword by Jeremy Barras ix

Preface xi

Note on the Translation and Transliteration xix

Acknowledgment xxi

Abbreviations xxiii

1. Introduction 3

2. *Vayishlach* 21

3. A *Peshat* Analysis of Israel 25

4. A *Remez* Analysis of Israel 40

5. A *Derash* Analysis of Israel 70

6. A *Sod* Analysis of Israel 87

7. New Age: The Number 2,701 and the Star of David 102

8. Contraction 119

Appendix 1 129

Appendix 2 134

Appendix 3 136

Appendix 4 138

Appendix 5 142

Appendix 6 143

Bibliography 145

Names Index 155

Subject Index 159

Foreword

How fortunate we are to welcome a fresh approach to the name Israel. As the author notes, the mission of this valuable addition aimed at increasing the reader's knowledge of Torah and appreciation for the name of today's Jewish people. Through clear investigation using the Pardes model (explained within), the reader is taken on a journey from the outer skin to the inner core of Israel's eternal significance.

The biblical nation of Israel is perhaps the world's only nation that has a homeland before it ever even arrives there. While the Book of Genesis details the lives of the patriarchs and matriarchs, it is not until the Book of Exodus when the Israelite nation blossoms into anything more than a small family clan. Born as a nation in exile, the Israelite nation experiences more than two centuries of bondage dreaming of one day returning to their homeland. This land, known as *Eretz Yisrael*, exists only in the consciousness of an enslaved nation. For the rest of the world, it is known as Canaan.

In the dream world of the Israelite slave is the vision of one day returning home to a land never before seen. That dream would include conquering the land and renaming it with the name Israel. In this exquisitely researched book, the author offers a new approach to understanding the nature of such a dream. Just as the Israelite slave in Egyptian bondage dreamed of a homeland within the borders of biblical Israel, so did the subscribers to the dream advanced by the Zionist Theodore Herzl. For each descendant of the sons of Jacob, the notion of Israel is more than just a homeland. It is even more than the essence of what is today known as a Jew. Israel is in fact the DNA of a people that was fashioned into the fabric of the world by its Creator. Those who recognize the Torah as the blueprint the Creator consulted when fashioning both the cosmic and human experience find evidence inscribed from the very first letter. This work will advance the reader's understanding of these concepts. Using the Pardes method, the author beautifully weaves a myriad of scholarly approaches that elucidate the meaning of the name Israel from every possible angle.

Israel was a person, a patriarch, and a place, *Eretz Yisrael.* This is indisputable from the biblical perspective. Nevertheless, to limit this name to a person, or even to a place, would be to disregard the core power and significance of the Creator's intention. At the very least, it would serve to ignore centuries of deep introspection into the core essence of a nation by its most illustrious scholars and leaders. In this book, Michael Alter will disabuse you of this approach, and take you on a journey into the mystical and spiritual power of a nation destined to bring knowledge of the Creator to our sub-lunar world. It is useful for the reader to carefully internalize the Pardes approach through the use of the preface and introduction, and then follow carefully through the book as the method builds from the opening peshat understanding to a crescendo of deep mystical investigation. On the course of this journey, the reader is aided by six carefully researched figures and eighteen tables that clearly synthesize rather complex materials.

As a rabbi among the people of Israel, this work serves to deepen my connection to every aspect of my tradition. It will further serve to bring new light into the academic and mystical understanding of the unique name of an eternal nation and will be a useful resource on the bookshelves of all rabbis, cantors, educators, and anyone understanding of the origins and deep meaning of the name and people of Israel. It is fitting that 100% of the proceeds of this work will be donated to academic and medical facilities in the modern State of Israel. The author has beautifully dedicated this work to the Jewish people in honor of Israel's 75th birthday. I am grateful to him for his generosity of spirit and dedication in responding to the spiritual and physical needs of the people of Israel.

JEREMY BARRAS
Senior Rabbi
Temple Beth Am, Miami, Florida

Preface

WHAT IS A NAME? Why is a name important? Names like words, conceal, and reveal. A name is a grouping of letters of an alphabet or other symbols. It represents the identification of a person or an object. Therefore, it is a word or set of words by which a person, animal, place, or thing is known, addressed, or refers. *The Concise Oxford English Dictionary* defines a name as follows.

name *noun*

1.   a word or set of words by which someone or something is known.

2.   a famous person.[2]

The Oxford English Dictionary lists the following, among its many definitions of the word "name":

1.1. a. *trans.* To give a name or names to (persons, places, things, etc.); to call by some name.

2.   a. To call by some title or epithet.

3.   To call (a person or thing) by the right name.[3]

Historically, names have served as fingerprint or retina scans of one's identity or a computer password. Judaism enhances this perspective. A name is pointedly central in Jewish tradition. The Jewish community knows numerous special events where names appear. Here are some examples.

When attending a *b'rit milah*
When attending a *simchat bat*
When a baby receives its name after birth
When a person receives their name after becoming Jewish by choice
When reciting the Shema twice each day (morning and evening)

2.   *The Concise Oxford English Dictionary*, 946.

3.   *The Oxford English Dictionary*, 204.

> When being called to the Torah for a *bar* or *bat mitzvah*
> When being called up to the Torah
> When requesting a *Mi Shebeirach* (blessing for healing)
> When signing a marriage contract (*kettubah*)
> When reciting a name during the *Yizkor* Memorial prayer
> When attending a funeral service
> When preparing a gravestone or reading a name on a gravestone
> When attending an unveiling (*Hakamat HaMatzevah*)
> When examining or making a family tree

The Torah states that "Israel" is a divinely given name and a divine creation.

> Genesis 35:9 *Then God appeared to Jacob again when he came from Paddan-aram, and He blessed him. 10 God said to him, "Your name is Jacob; You shall no longer be called Jacob, But Israel shall be your name." So He called him Israel.* (NASB)

The kabbalistic literature discusses and explores God's means of creation. According to tradition, God created the world through the use of the Hebrew alphabet via divine speech/utterances: "*And God said* [*va'yomer*], (Genesis 1:3, 6, 9, 11, 14, 20, 24, 26, and 28). Nine acts of creation described in Genesis 1:1–2:4 employ the introductory words, "*And God said.*" If we include the first word of the Torah, *Bereshit* ("*In the beginning of*"), being a divine utterance, we can say that the universe came into being via ten utterances. This teaching is found in Avot 5:1. "By ten sayings the world was created" (e.g., Bereshit Rabbah 17:1; Megillah 21b:9. Avot of Rabbi Nathan 31:2; Rabbeinu Yonah on Avot 5:1). Thus, God's speech is metaphorically the means of His creation and sustenance. Rabbi Ariel Bar Tzadok elaborates.

> How did Hashem create the universe? What vehicle or method did He chose to use in order to manifest Being? The Torah itself answers us quite clearly. G-d spoke, and what He spoke came into being, Creation was brought about by speech. Yet, G-d forbid that we would ever interpret a Biblical metaphor literally. G-d has no form or semblance of form. Thus, He has no mouth with which to speak in a literal sense.[4]

This concept repeats in the Psalms.

> Psalm 33:6 *By the word of the LORD the heavens were made, And by the breath of His mouth all their lights.* (NASB)

---

4. Bar Tzadok, *Walking in the Fire*, 369.

Psalm 33:9 *For He spoke, and it was done;*
He commanded, and it stood firm. (NASB)

This thought is in the Hebrew word (employed by magicians): *Abracadabra*. Rabbi Bar Tzadok points out that this Hebrew word is a Hebrew phrase, which means: "I create (*A'bra*) what (*ca*) I speak (*dab'ra*)."[5] This idea is also tersely mentioned in the Talmud, Berakhot 55a: "Rab Judah said in the name of Rab: Bezalel knew how to combine the letters by which the heavens and earth were created." Commentators assign mystical powers to the letters of the Hebrew alphabet. In this case, Bezalel knew the art of combining sacred letters.

The first verse of the Bible provides a "hint" that the letters of the Hebrew alphabet were "metaphorical tools" employed during the creation process. It contains seven Hebrew words. Take the first letter of each word and add its numerical value (*gematria*). The result is *Bet* (2) + *Bet* (2) + *Aleph* (1) +*Aleph* (1) + *He* (5) + *Vav* (6) + *He* (5), which equals twenty-two (22). Altogether, there are twenty-two letters in the Hebrew alphabet.

Sefer Yetzirah (*the Book of Formation or Book of Creation*) is one of the oldest and most mysterious kabbalistic texts. The opening of this profound text reads as follows.

> Yah, the Lord of hosts, the living God, King of the Universe, Omnipotent, All-Kind and Merciful, Supreme and Extolled, who is Eternal, Sublime and Most-Holy, ordained (formed) and created the Universe in thirty-two mysterious paths of wisdom by three Sepharim, namely: 1) S'for סְפָר (2 ;) Sippur סִפּוּר; and 3) Sapher סֵפֶר which are in Him one and the same.[6]

God's speech is not only the metaphorical means of His creation and the modality of its continued sustenance. If God were to stop speaking, the universe would return to nothingness.[7]

I once heard, "in Hebrew, a name is not merely a convenient conglomeration of letters. It is profoundly spiritual. Besides, the name reveals a person's essential characteristic." Ronald Eisenberg, writing in *The JPS Guide to Jewish Traditions*, echoes these thoughts when he states, "A person's name

---

5. Bar Tzadok, *Walking in Fire*, 371.

6 Kalisch, *Sefer Yetzirah*, 11. Translators provide differing translations and explanations of three keywords. For instance, in his commentary, Aryeh Kaplan elaborates on the words: *Sepher*, with text; *Sephar*, with number; and *Sippur* with communication.

7. See Shneur Zalman, *Tanya, Shaar Hayichud*, 7.

is thought to define and control his or her soul and destiny (*Berakhot* 7b). Therefore, the selection of an appropriate name is a critical decision."[8]

Harry Waton wrote the following insights.

> The Hebrew word for name is: שם, and its numerical value is 340. 340 is also the numerical value of the word: ספר—book. A book reveals the thoughts of an author. The thoughts of an author are revealed through the book; the book reveals explicitly what is implicit in the mind of the author. To name a thing is to make manifest explicitly what is implicit in the nature of the thing. The letters of the Hebrew alphabet symbolize profound ideas, and the names of the letters manifest the ideas which are implicit in the letters themselves.[9]

Rabbi Benjamin Blech and his wife, Elaine Blech, published another relevant text, *Your Name Is Your Blessing: Hebrew Names and Their Mystical Meanings*. In the preface, they add an essential consideration.

> A name is a book. It captures a person's character and personality. It describes everyone's mission on earth. It contains a prophecy as well as a powerful, potential blessing. It is the only possession we have that remains with us even after death. For a parent, it is the most valuable gift we can ever give to a child.[10]

Later, in the section "Your Name Is Your Neshama—The Key to Your Soul," they add these words.

> The Hebrew for "name" is שם *shem*. These two Hebrew letters, ש (*sin*) and מ (*mem*) are central to the word *neshamah*— נשמה — the Hebrew word for "soul." The soul, or essence, of any human being is contained in his or her name.

According to tradition, names given to children after birth are not accidental or coincidental. Naming a baby is power and responsibility. Giving names is profound, as demonstrated in Genesis. A name is a key to one's *nefesh* (soul). Again, it is noteworthy that the middle two letters of the word *neshama* are *shin* and *mem*. These two letters spell the Hebrew word *shem* (name).

Interestingly, Rabbi Moshe Wisnefsky translates and adapts from *Sefer ha-Likutim* (published in "*Apples from the Orchard*"), the numerical value of "*nefesh*" is the same as that of the two names, Abraham and Jacob together.

8. Eisenberg, *The JPS Guide*, 14.

9. Waton, *The Key to the Bible*, 23.

10. Blech and Blech, *Your Name Is Your Blessing*, ix.

Nefesh: *nun-pe-shin* = 50 + 80 + 300 = 430.

Abraham: *aleph-bet-resh-he-mem* = 1 + 2 + 200 + 5 + 40 = 248

Jacob (in Hebrew, "*Yaakov*"): *yod-ayin-qoph-bet* = 10 + 70 + 100 + 2 = 182.

248 + 182 = 430.[11]

Tradition instructs us that our children's names result from a partnership between our efforts and the response of God. However, Ecclesiastes Rabbah adds an important dimension: "Everyone has three names: the name given by parents, the name others call one, and the name one earns."

This text divides into eight chapters, plus the front and back matter. The front matter includes a table of contents, preface, and acknowledgments.

Chapter 1 is the Introduction. It provides historical references to the name Israel. Afterward, there is a discussion of the purpose and limitations of the book. Next, the chapter engages with and explains the system of *pardes*: *peshat, remez, derash,* and *sod.* Two of these methods—*remez* and *sod*—are elaborated further in the text. The examination of *remez* includes six methods of *gematria. Gematria* helps us interpret one or several words under a set system employing numerical values. The numbers 10, 26, 32, 70, 73, and 541 are especially significant. In the course of covering the various *remez* interpretations, this text explores a variety of topics:

(1) the shape and size of the letters

(2) permutations and anagrams of Israel

Afterward, our examination of the method of *sod* contains a discussion of the Four World System and the ten *sefirot.*

Chapter 2 examines *Parashah Vayishlach.* It discusses and provides a brief overview of the eighth weekly Torah reading. Twice in the weekly Torah reading of *Parashah Vayishlach* (Genesis 32:4–36:43), the origin of the name "Israel" appears:

Genesis 32: 25–31

Genesis 35: 9–10

Chapter 3 is "A *Peshat* Analysis of Israel." This chapter presents traditional sources (midrash and the Talmud), biblical commentators from Rashi to Robert Alter, and contemporary writers. Collectively, thirty-one readings are present with extracts from additional sources.

Each issue usually opens with the name of the work or identifies its author. What follows is either an excerpt or a complete quote. Footnotes

11. Wisnefsky, *Apples from the Orchard.*

incorporate (1) identification of the source of the material (i.e., the author, short title, and page number(s) and (2), if necessary, additional explanatory information such as terminology. In the interests of completeness, readers are encouraged to go back and examine the entire source material.

Chapter 4 is devoted to a *remez* analysis of Israel. First, it explores several topics found throughout much of this book. Excerpts by nine of seventeen writers discuss the shape and size of the letters found in the name Israel and *Bereshit* (the first word of the Torah). There are extracts and elaborations from additional sources. Afterward, there is a brief analysis of the permutations of the letters in the name Israel. Next, we explore the subject of anagrams. Three readings, including one table, are provided. The spiritual DNA of the Jewish people is visible in Table 5. Sources span over one thousand years. Sub-sections include the following.

4.3—*Gematria*: The Numerical Value of the First Letter of Israel: Ten

4.4—*Gematria*: The Numerical Value of the First Letter and Last Letter of Israel: Forty

4.5—*Gematria*: The Number Twenty-six and the Concealment of God's Name

4.6—*Gematria*: The Numerical Value of the First and Last Letter of the Torah Equal Thirty-Two. Eight readings with helpful useful notes are presented, dealing with that number.

4.7—*Gematria*: The Seventy Names of Israel. Here, two readings are presented, with two supplements in the appendix.

4.8—*Gematria*: This section deals with the significant number: 541, the standard numerical value of Israel. Eighteen readings comprise this sub-section. Excerpts include Abraham Abulafia to contemporary writers exemplified by Rabbi Yitzchak Ginsburgh. It also incorporates two tables. One of the fascinating insights concealed in the numerical value of Israel is the means of its redemption from Egyptian slavery. This significant reading will provide readers with spiritual enlightenment, especially during Pesach.

Chapter 5 is titled "A *Derash* Analysis of Israel." Thirty-two readings, several secondary sources, and one figure are present. These readings include sources from Midrash Rabbah, Abraham Abulafia, Rabbi Eleazar ben Judah of Worms, Gershom Scholem, the late Rabbi Jonathan Sacks, and contemporary writers such as Rabbi Matitahu Glazerson and Rabbi Aaron L. Raskin.

Chapter 6 is "A *Sod* Analysis of Israel." Eighteen readings comprise this chapter, along with additional excerpted comments. Extensively, these readings discuss the ten *sefirot*, "the 231 gates" (*Sefer Yetzirah*), and the Agent of Intellect. Several sources include *Sefer Yetzirah*, the *Zohar*, and writers such as Rabbi Ya'avetz of Emden and Rabbi Aryeh Kaplan. This chapter incorporates one figure.

Chapter 7 is titled "New Age: The Number 2,701 and the Star of David." The number 2,701 is interrelated to Israel, the Star of David (i.e., the Magen David), the first verse of the Torah, and creation. In recent years, mathematicians and physicists employing computer technology have built on the knowledge of their predecessors. This chapter explores topics related to triangular numbers, prime numbers, and star hexagram numbers. Assisting the reader are five tables and three figures.

Controversy exists about the Star of David (the Magen David). Is it a Jewish symbol? When and where did it originate in Jewish usage? Is it kabbalistic? This chapter explores these and other subjects, bringing together readings from both sides of the intellectual aisle. This section includes insightful and practical information for clergy and educators working with children and teenagers.

Chapter 8 is "Contraction." Here, we combine (contract) and discuss the material covered earlier in this book. First, twelve interconnecting points are the subject of focus. Inside sub-section 8.2, "The First Word of the Torah and the Creation Process: *Bereshit*," is reviewed and further explored. Topics include divine speech and the word *Hokhmah*. We re-explore and expand facts about the numbers 2,701, 37, 73, 541, and 703. Afterward, we reexamine the subjects, "The end of the action was at first in thought," and unique features (and hints) of the letters forming the name Israel. In sub-section 8.6, we again explore the Star of David (Magen David). Last, sub-section 8.7 is the Conclusion.

The back matter consists of a six-part appendix, name, and subject index. The appendix is relevant, and I urge readers to peruse it. Here, the reader has presented an alternative when reading these sections (appendix 1). These readings correspond to and parallel the traditional Jewish life cycle stages. The reader is encouraged to develop meaningful parallels and examine the index list of names ending in *El* [appendix 3 and 4].

This preface includes several thoughts mentioned in two earlier texts by this author. First, while researching material for this text, the author was surprised to find extensive writing on the subject of names. However, it would be difficult for laypeople to extract all this information from the numerous works on the subject because many are in various languages. Translated works contain literature from many different genres (e.g., the

Hebrew Bible, Talmudic, midrashim, kabbalistic, Chasidic philosophy, and general commentary). Thus, this book aims to bring into one volume a representative selection of works spanning over 3500 years, addressing several questions: What is the meaning of the name "Israel," and what concealed spiritual insights are within that divine name?

Contemporary readers, both Jewish (especially those who are less observant or secular) and non-Jewish, may take exception to some statements in this text. Claims that the Jews are the "chosen people" and that Israel is "the purpose of creation" may be viewed as obsolete, ethnocentric, and possibly offensive. The sources of these excerpts span vast areas of geography and history. Additionally, they are the products of many different cultures, societies, environments, and times. The interpretations of statements change over time and within different cultures. Hopefully, the presentation of this multiplicity of views will be beneficial to those who read it.

This reference text is intended primarily for the use of educated laypeople, educators, and clergy. However, as well, it will be beneficial to other readers, including those who are non-Jewish. Furthermore, this text is mostly a wide-ranging anthology of almost 150 works, many of which are translations. No matter how meticulously prepared, translations cannot do justice to the original. Idiomatic terms and expressions, for example, often lose nuances of meaning in translation. Furthermore, the precise meaning of a text may be lost when its translator attempts to preserve the author's original style. The reader is therefore encouraged to take these facts into careful consideration.

This text demonstrates that the library of Jewish writings on Israel's name is voluminous; and that many interpretations exist. Besides, many of the concepts are esoteric and difficult to understand. If the readers find some terms unfamiliar, they should refer either to the footnotes or standard reference works for further elucidation. However, another possible solution to this reality is found in the Mishnah: "Provide yourself with a teacher and avoid doubt" (Avot 1:16).

Note on the Translation
and Transliteration

The English translation and transliteration of Hebrew names and words vary according to tradition and source. Some transliterations follow Ashkenazi and Yiddish traditions; others, the Sephardic. Israel, for example, is the conventional English spelling found in the *Encyclopedia Judaica* and Jewish Publication Society. However, elsewhere, the name is Yisrael, Y'srael, Ysrael, or Yisroel. The divergent spellings for personal names, names of letters in the Hebrew alphabet, the ten *sefirot*, and Hebrew words (*Bereshit, Bereshis, B'reshit, B'reshith, Bereishees*) represent quotations from the source.

Acknowledgment

Virtually all books are a team project.

I wish to acknowledge the efforts of production manager, Matthew Wimer; cover designer, Jonathan Hill; typesetter, Savanah N. Landerholm; and all other Wipf and Stock staff members for their helpfulness throughout the production of this text. I also thank Senior Rabbi, Jeremy Barras, Temple Beth Am, for graciously writing the Foreword. In addition, this book stands on the shoulders of the cited sages, commentators, and translators (especially Eliyahu Munk and Akiva Roth). With their cumulative contribution, this text was possible.

Abbreviations

BCE	before the common era
ca.	circa, around
CE	common era
cf.	"compare" or "see, by way of comparison"
Dan	Daniel
Deut	Deuteronomy
Diss.	dissertation
Eccl	Ecclesiastes
ed.(s)	editor(s), edited by
e.g.	*exempli gratia*, for example
esp.	especially
Exod	Exodus
Esth	Esther
Ez or Ezek	Ezekiel
fr.	From
Hos	Hosea
i.e.	*id est*, that is
Isa	Isaiah
Gen	Genesis
1–2 Chr	Chronicles
JBL	*Journal of Biblical Literature*
Jer	Jeremiah

Josh	Joshua
Kgs	1–2 Kings
Maimonides	Moses ben Maimon
Nachmanides	Moses ben Nahman
NASB	*New American Standard Bible*
N.B.	*note bene*, note carefully
n.d.	no date
Neh	Nehemiah
NJPS	*Tanakh: The Holy Scriptures: The New JPS Translation According to the Traditional Hebrew Text*
p. or pp.	page(s)
par.	paragraph
Ps	Psalm
Rashbam	Rabbi Samuel ben Meir
Rashi	Rabbi Solomon ben Isaac
vol	volume
v(v).	verse(s)
Zech	Zechariah
Zeph	Zephaniah

Genesis 35: 9 *Then God appeared to Jacob again when he came from Paddan-aram, and He blessed him. 10 God said to him, "Your name is Jacob; You shall no longer be called Jacob, But Israel shall be your name." So He called him Israel.* (NASB)

1.

Introduction

ISRAEL IS A MOMENTOUS, divinely given biblical name. Evan-Shoshan's *Concordance* reports that "Israel" appears in the Hebrew Bible 2,510 times.[1] A different tabulation is in appendix 2.

The name Israel appears in several applications.

I.   An individual, the grandson of Abraham (Avraham), son of Isaac (Yitzchak), and the father of twelve sons and one daughter. He is also one of the patriarchs.

 1. It is the second name for Jacob (Ya'akov), announced presumably by an angel (Genesis 32:29) and later explicitly by God after his wrestling match at Peniel (Genesis 35:9–10). Therefore, Israel is a divine name.

II. A people:

 2. It is the name of the descendants of Jacob. Frequently, in Scripture, it is designated *B'nei Yisrael* (the children of Israel), or less commonly, *Goy Kadosh* (Holy Nation or people, Exodus 19:6).

 3. Yisrael or Israelite: Generally, any member of *K'lal Yisrael* (congregation of Israel), but in the specific sense, one who is neither *Kohen* nor of the tribe of *Levi*, thus not a descendant of the tribe of Levi.

 4. The name Israel is designated a spiritual entity that transcends political boundaries. Israel is "God's chosen people," a people related uniquely to YHVH, "the God of Israel," in a covenant-based sacred bond that

1. Even-Shoshan, ed. *A New Concordance of the Bible*, 513.

goes back at least to the sacred tribal relationship established under Joshua, as reported in Joshua 24. They are also designated to be a holy nation (Exodus 19:6) and holy people (Leviticus 19:6), as well as a kingdom of priests (Exodus 19:6).

III.   A nation:

5. It is the nation that descended from Jacob.

6. It refers to the name given to the northern kingdom of the ten tribes under Jeroboam.

7. It refers to a nation from the Babylonian exile.

8. It is the modern state of Israel, established in 1948.

IV.   Geography/Land: It refers to a land called "*Eretz Yisrael,*" located south of Lebanon, north of Egypt, and west of modern-day Jordan.

9. Geopolitically, it is a gateway and land bridge to three continents: Africa, Asia, and Europe.

This land is also of theological significance.

10. It is where Abram offered Isaac as an offering to God.

11. It is the Promised Land.

12. It is the site of the holy Temple.

13. It is where the Messiah will be born.

> Midrash Tanhuma, Kedoshim 10: Just as the navel is set in the middle of a person, so the Land of Israel is the navel of the world. Thus it is stated (in Ezek. 38:12), "*who dwell on the navel of the earth.*" And the foundation of the world comes out of it, as stated (*Ps.* 50:1), "*A psalm of Asaph. God, the Lord God spoke and summoned the world from East to West.*" How is this known? (Ps. 50:2), "*Out of Zion God has shined forth as the perfection of beauty.*" The Land of Israel sits at the center of the world; Jerusalem is in the center of the Land of Israel; the sanctuary is in the center of Jerusalem; the Temple building is in the center of the sanctuary; the ark is in the center of the Temple building; and the foundation stone, out of which the world was founded, is before the Temple.[2]

2. Midrash Tanhuma, "Leviticus 19:23."

> Pesiqta de-Rab Kahana 26:4 (Mandelbaum ed.)
>
> As the navel is set in the middle of a person so is Israel the navel of the world, as it is said: *That dwell in the navel of the earth* (Ezek. 38:12). The Land of Israel is located in the center of the world, Jerusalem in the center of the Land of Israel, the Temple in the center of Jerusalem, the *heikhal* in the center of the Temple, the ark in the center of the *heikhal*, and in front of the *heikhal* is the even shetiyyah [foundation stone] from which the world was started.[3]

In brief, the name Israel refers to a: (1) person, (2) distinctive people, (3) a definite nation, or (4) a unique piece of land.[4]

Previously, the thinking was that the first archaeological and textual reference to Israel was the Stele of Merneptah. In 1896, Flinders Petrie at Thebes discovered it. The stele, set up by Amenhotep III, is a sizeable granite work over ten feet high. The inscription dates from approximately the fifth year of Merneptah's reign (1220 BCE). The stele refers to the numerous victories of the Pharaoh over several people. The relevant sentence reads as follows.

> Wasted is Tehenu, Kheta is pacified, Pekanan is captured with every evil circumstance, Ashalon is carried captive, Gezer is taken, Yenoam is brought to nought, Israel is destroyed, its seed is not, Syria has become as the widows of Egypt, all the lands together are at peace.[5]

It is currently housed in the Egyptian Museum in Cairo.

Herschel Shanks, Wolfgang Zwickel, and Pieter van der Veen challenge traditional thinking.[6] The latter writes these words.

> Several years ago [the late] Manfred Görg proposed to read a fragmentarily preserved topographical or regional name as Israel on a stone relief now kept at the store rooms of the New Museum in Berlin (ÄM 21687) ... New research during the last number of years has confirmed this reading, although the writing of the name is different from that of the Merenptah

---

3. Ulmer, "The Jerusalem Temple in Pesiqta Rabbati," 231–32.

4. Harvey discusses thirteen different groups or phrases for Israel in ancient Jewish literature. See Harvey, "The True Israel Uses of the Names Jew, Hebrew and Israel," 110–54.

5. Jack, "The Israel Stele of Merenptah," 40–44.

6. Shanks, "When did ancient Israel begin?," 59–62, 67; Zwickel and van der Veen, "The earliest reference to Israel," 129–40.

inscription. Some characteristics appear to demonstrate that this inscription is older than the Israel stela of Merenptah and may likely date to the 14th or earlier 13th century BCE.

Unfortunately, the stone is damaged, with 2/3rds of the inscription remaining. Nonetheless, Görg read the name Israel. Zwickel and van der Veen said, "an increasing number of scholars now tend to accept this reading (most recently so Wimmer 2014, XVII)." However, they also add, "Likely it will never be possible to completely ascertain this reading, but it is at least a convincing proposal, which deserves to be taken seriously by Egyptologists, Old Testament exegetes and ancient historians alike."

The name's etymology has been subject to an extensive and ongoing debate without resolution. In many ways, investigators study this topic: linguistic (e.g., Akkadian, Arabic, Aramean, Egyptian), historical, socio-political, exegetical, and theological points of view. The literature is reasonably robust. Three linguistic journal articles are cited frequently in the literature. Eduard Sachsse, W.F. Albright, and Robert Coote are the authors.[7] Occasionally, it will be necessary to briefly re-explore those approaches.

1.1. PURPOSE OF THE BOOK

The purpose of this book is to present the reader with an investigation via *pardes* (פרדס) of the name "Israel."[8] This study will primarily incorporate Jewish sources, both dated and current.[9]

1.2. LIMITATIONS

This investigation will not extensively delve into the etymological arguments about the name's origin. Sachsse and Albright have already, in-depth, completed that task. Standard dictionaries and lexicons have sufficiently

---

7. Sachsse, "Die Etymolgie" 1–15; Albright, The Names "Israel" and "Judah," 151; Cote, "The Meaning of the name Israel," 137–42. Also examine: Kogan, "The Etymology of Israel," 3: 237–55; Marcus, "The Hebrew Sibilant *sin*," 141–50.

8. Additionally, this text is to honor the State of Israel on its Diamond Jubilee anniversary (75th) and contribute all royalties to American Friends of ALYN Hospital and the American Technion Society.

9. Several informative encyclopedia entries include: Stamm, "Names," 764–66; Jacobs, "Names (Personal)," 9:152–60; Cheyne, "Jacob," "Name," 3: 2264–370; 'Names," 3: 2371–3331. Also see Ganoune Diop, The Name "Israel" and Related Expressions.

analyzed that topic.[10] In his doctoral dissertation, G.A. Danell identified eight different roots of just the first part of the name ישראל. They are

1. שרה to fight

2. שרה to preserve, persist

3. שרה to shine

4. שרה (or שרר) to rule, dominate

5. שׂר׳ to heal (the sick)

6. שׂר׳ to be straight, upright

7. אשׂר to be happy; the name of the god and the tribe Asher belongs here too.

8. *iser*, an Aegean root with the significance 'holy.'[11]

Louis Ginzberg discusses additional explanations for the name:

1. יש + אל = "trying to sing instead of the angels" or "joyful like the angels at the time of their singing,"

2. שאר אל = "the remnant of God," and

3. ישר אל = "he who walks straight with the Lord."[12]

Robert Coughenour offers yet another possibility. He writes this suggestion.

> The Hebrew name is a clause formed of two Hebrew words. The "-el" ending is the name of God in Semitic languages and indicates the subject of the clause. The verbal predicate is the imperfect form of a verb, *sārāh*, meaning probably, "to rule." Thus the name Israel means "God rules."[13]

Additionally, this book will not investigate the documentary hypothesis as a possible explanation for the origin of the name. Furthermore, in general, we will not discuss various rationales why Jacob's name is changed twice. However, it would be remiss not to mention a midrashic and rabbinic comment.

> Midrash Rabbah (ca. 500 CE)
>
> *Vayishlach* (78.3)

---

10. Cheyne, "Jacob," 2:2311; Gerleman, "Israel," 581–84; Zobel, "yiśîraʾel," 6: 397–420.

11. Danell, *Studies in the Name of Israel*, 22–23.

12. Ginzberg, *The Legends of the Jews*, 5:307.

13. Coughenour, "A Conversation on Israel," 17.

[No, for] it was taught: It was not intended that the name of Jacob should disappear, but that 'Israel' should be the principal name and 'Jacob' is a secondary one. R. Zechariah interpreted it in R. Aha's name: At all events, '*Thy name is Jacob,*' save that, *But Israel* [too] *shall be thy name* (Gen. XXXV, 10): Jacob would be the principal name—'Israel' was added to it.[14]

Rabbi Bahya ben Asher (1255—1340)

Midrash Rabbeinu Bachya Torah Commentary

Genesis 47:29 From a more rational or scientific point of view we may detect a distinct pattern in the Torah sometimes choosing to refer to Yaakov by his original name and sometimes by his additional name. The name Yaakov applies to the physical part of Yaakov's personality, matters connected to his terrestrial existence, whereas the name Israel refers to spiritual aspects of his personality, matters connected to his eternal existence in celestial regions.[15]

1.3. EXPLANATION OF PARDES (PARDES)

Pardes (*PaRDeS*; פרדס) is the Hebrew word for "garden" or "orchard." The English term paradise (PaRaDiSe) derives from the same Persian root. This word, formed by the initials of four other words, is an acronym. The first letter of each of the four words (i.e., *P-R-D-S*) is employed, and the addition of vowels for pronunciation, giving, *pardes*. Like the layers of an onion, each layer is more intense than the last. Similarly, tasting an orchard's fruit, the benefits are experienced on many levels.

In *Language, Eros, Being*, Elliot Wolfson offers a helpful description.

The four levels are presented sequentially as stages of ever-increasing disclosure, the first offered through the barrier of a wall, the second from behind a curtain, the third through a more subtle screen, and finally, the fourth, ostensibly clearing away all obstructions; the reader encounters the text face-to-face, which in zoharic idiom signifies union of the most intimate source.[16]

In rabbinic Judaism or the interpretation of a text in Torah study, *pardes* refers to four approaches to biblical exegesis. The earliest reference to

14. Freedman, *Midrash Rabbah: Genesis*, 2:717.

15. Asher, *Midrash Rabbeinu Bachya*, 683. The same idea is found earlier on page 531 (Genesis 35:10).

16. Wolfson, *Language, Eros, Being*, 223.

the four levels is in the *Midrash ha-Ne'elam* to the book of Ruth.[17] Scholars suggest the *Midrash ha-Ne'elam* is the oldest constituent of the *Zohar*, one of the chief texts in Jewish mysticism. In that text, the fourfold scheme is related to a nut: "Just as a nut has an outer shell and a kernel, each word of the Torah contains an outward fact ('*ma'aseh*'), midrash, *haggadah*, and mystery (*sod*), each of which is deeper in meaning than the preceding."[18] Three of the earliest kabbalistic writers who discussed and utilized this scheme were Moses de Leon, Bahya ben Asher, and Joseph Gikatilla.

Proverbs 25:11 is a well-known passage translated from Hebrew to English in several ways. A frequent version is: "there are 'apples of gold' hidden behind the 'silver filigree' of the surface text. Another stated, "*A word fitly spoken is like apples of gold encased or in settings of silver*" (*ketapuhei zahav b'maskiyyoth shel kesef*). Maimonides, on Proverbs, explains in his *Guide to the Perplexed.*

> A word fitly spoken is like apples of gold in vessels of silver.
>
> Hear the explanation of what he said; —the word *maskiyoth*, the Hebrew equivalent for "vessels," denotes "filigree network"— i.e., things in which there are very small apertures, such as are frequently wrought by silversmiths. They are called in Hebrew *maskiyoth* (lit. "transpicuous," from the verb *sakah*, "he saw" a root which occurs also in the Targum of Onkelos, Genesis 26:8) because the eye penetrates through them. Thus Solomon meant to say, "*just as apples of gold in silver filigree with small apertures, so is a word fitly spoken.*"
>
> See how beautifully the conditions of a good simile are described in this figure! It shows that in every word which has a double sense, a literal one and a figurative one, the plain meaning must be as valuable as silver, and the hidden meaning still more precious; so that the figurative meaning bears the same relation to the literal one as gold to silver. It is further necessary that the plain sense of the phrase shall give to those who consider it some notion of that which the figure represents. Just as a golden apple overlaid with a network of silver, when seen at a distance, or looked at superficially, is mistaken for a silver apple, but when a keen-sighted person looks at the object well, he will find what is within and see that the apple is gold. The same is the case with the figures employed by prophets.[19]

---

17. Scholem, *On the Kabbalah*, 54.

18. Scholem, *On the Kabbalah*, 54.

19. Maimonides, *The Guide of the Perplexed*, 6.

A word or text has a dual meaning: literal (silver) and figurative (gold). Therefore, when viewed below (the overlay), the apple is exposed as gold, which is more precious than silver—so too are words.

> Rav Shimon bar Yochai said (*Zohar Chadash*, Tikunim II:93b, Zohar III:152a) "Woe are those whose hearts are stuffed and whose eyes are closed! So many secrets are hidden in the Torah, and they pay no attention to them. They only want to eat the "straw" of the Torah—the simple meaning, or the "garment" of the Torah. They don't taste from the deep intellect which it contains within."

Lastly, it is frequently noteworthy that commentators incorporate more than one approach when analyzing a word or verse. Therefore, at times, this blending methodology requires a subjective classification.

Following is an exploration of the four-fold methodology of biblical exegesis and interpretation of the name Israel. Study and learn.

1.4. PESHAT

פ *Peshat* (פשט) refers to the contextual, plain, or simple meaning of a Scriptural passage. Its description is the surface meaning of the text. Literal is an inaccurate translation. In contrast, *peshat* correctly means the intended, the explicit meaning. Rashi (1040–1105), perhaps the foremost Jewish biblical commentator, primarily wrote at this level. As a general rule, the extended meaning never contradicts the basic meaning. The Talmud states that no passage loses its *peshat*: Talmud Shabbat 63a—"Rabbi Kahana objected to Mar son of Rabbi Huna: But this refers to the words of the Torah? A verse cannot depart from its plain meaning, he replied."

Moshe Idel elaborates a discussion explaining the importance of *peshat*, yet, a paradox about its limitation for understanding a text.

> A pun related to the word *pardes* will easily illustrate this. R. Hayyim Yoseph David Azulai, better known as HYDA', commented in his *Midbar Oedeimot*: "Whoever believes only in the plain sense of the Bible, *peshat*, is indeed a fool, as a permutation of the consonants of *peshat* 'demonstrates': *tipesh*." Moreover, he continues, without the secret, namely the Kabbalistic interpretation, designated by the *s* in *pardes*, the three first consonants of this word would form the word *pered*, an ass. Important as the first three methods may be for the accomplished Kabbalist, in themselves they do not suffice for the real understanding of the

text. In fact, without the knowledge of the Kabbalah the exegete is no more than an ass.[20]

1.5. REMEZ

ר *Remez* (רמז), in modern Hebrew, means "hint." In a biblical study, *remez* refers to alluded meaning, implied meaning, or the interpretation of Scripture at the level of allusive implication. This method explores the allegoric or symbolic meaning, often just beyond the literal sense. There exist, in fact, numerous types of *remez*. Two common forms of *remez* include "*notarikon*" (making words from letters taken from the beginning, middle, or end of the words in a sentence) and "*temurah*" (a technique used for the permutation of letters, where the letters in a word or phrase exchange with others). Many of the explanations in the Talmud focus on rather obvious and not-so-apparent hints in the Torah. Additional examples of *remez* include examining the number of letters in a word, the shape of the letters, the size of the letters, the oversized letters, the small letters, the crowns (*tagin*) above the letters, the vowels (*niqqud* or *nikud*), the spacing between words and letters, and even the white space that encompasses the black form of the letters.

For example, Rabbi Michael Munk discusses a connection between the name of God and Israel in his text. Both begin with the letter *yod*. The Tetragrammaton, the ineffable Divine Four-Letter Name of God, is YHVH. Noteworthy, the Jewish people are known by *four* names. They are the following:

יעקב		= Yaakov (Jacob)
ישראל		= Ysrael (Israel)
יהדה		= Yehudah (Judah)
ישרון		= Yeshurun (Jeshurun)[21]

Rabbi Moshe Cordovero, a 16th-century kabbalist, writing *Or Neerav* (Part V, Chapter 2), comments:

> [Thus] For you have no word or letter in the Torah that does not contain lofty mysteries.
>
> Happy is the portion of those who know it.
>
> If one should ask this question of a grammarian, he would answer that [the preceding examples] are among the letters that are [seemingly] superfluous. In our opinion, one who says that

20. Idel, *Absorbing Perfections*, 432.
21. Munk, *The Wisdom in the Hebrew Alphabet*, 129.

there is a superfluous [*yeter*] letter in the Torah should have his teeth taken out [*yutru*] if [he says it] deliberately. If [he says it] in error, then his Master will forgive him.[22]

According to the *Tikkunei Zohar* (70, 129a, b), the letters of the He-brew alphabet are vessels that receive their light from the *niqqud* (vowels). Vowels appear as dots or lines. Adding a vowel to the letter is likened to bringing life to an empty vessel (the body of the letter) and animating it. Therefore, the vowels give a soul to the letters. Furthermore, each vowel is associated with a *sefirah* and *gematria* (numerical value). One method of *gematria* employs the number ten for each dot (just like the letter *yod*, which has a numerical value of ten) and a six for a line (that resembles a *vav* and has the value of six). A search of the literature did not locate a discussion of the name Israel and its five vowels (*niqqud*): *hireq* (*chirik*), *shewa* (*sh'va*), *holam* (*cholem*), *qamets* (*kametz*), and *tsere* (*tzerey*).

The letter *yod* of Yisrael has a dot, a *hireq* below. Rabbi Aaron Raskin comments that the vowel refers to the *sefirah* of *Netzach*—victory and has the numerical value of ten. The letter *yod* also has the numerical value of ten.[23]

Open to speculation is that the sum numerical value of Israel's five vowels: *hireq* (10), *shewa* (20), *holam* (10), *qamets* (16), and *tsere* (20) totals seventy-six (76). In one type of *gematria*, seven plus six equals thirteen. That number coincides with the total number of male and female children of the patriarch, Israel. This methodology of *gematria* is called the "small" numerical value, or *"Mispar Katan"/ "Mispar Katari."* The numerical value is reduced by adding the numbers in the various digit placements. Thus, for example, the *Mispar Katan* of the numbers 76 and 3,280 are thirteen.

Another "conjecture," also employing *remez*, focuses on Genesis 46:26. That verse reports, "*All the people belonging to Jacob* [Israel], *who came to Egypt, his direct descendants, not including the wives of Jacob's* [Israel's] *sons, were sixty-six persons in all.*" (NASB) When Jacob's family traveled to Egypt, they literally "descended" geographically southward and to a place spiritually fallen. If we sum the numerical value of Israel's four "lowest" vowels: *hireq* (10), *shewa* (20), *qamets* (16), and *tsere* (20), the total is sixty-six (66). That number precisely totals the number of descendants from Ja-cob/Israel who descended to the lowest depths of Egypt.

Gematria (numerology) is perhaps the most extensive form of *re-mez*. It, accordingly, has and deserves extra attention and elaboration.[24]

---

22. Cordovero, *Introduction to Kabbalah*, 106.

23. Raskin, *Letters of Light*, 240.

24. Asher, *Perush Ba'al ha-Turim*; Ginsburgh, *The Hebrew Letters*; Glazerson, *Letters of Fire*; Haralick, *The Inner Meaning*; Locks, *Spice of Torah: Gematria*; Munk, *The Wisdom*

A haggadic hermeneutical rule for interpreting the Torah is the *Baraita of 32 Rules*, no. 29. It explains a word or group of words according to the letter's numerical value or by substituting other letters of the alphabet following a set system. The most numerous methods of calculation are in an anonymous manuscript (MS) No, 1822/MS Mich #460 [Part 123, f. 141–146] of the Bodleian Library, where there is a listing of seventy-five different forms of *gematria*. Several well-known methods of *gematria* are in tables 1 and 2.

1. The Standard value (*Mispar Ragil*)

2. The Absolute value (*Mispar Hekrehi*)

3. The Ordinal Value (*Mispar Sidduri*)

4. The Numerical Value of the Names of the Letters (*Mispar Shemi* or *Millui*)

5. Adding the Sum-Total of the Word; the Number of Letters in the Word (*Mispar Musaphi*)

6. The Reduce Value (*Mispar Katan*) (See tables 1–4)

Gutman Locks writes

> Gematria is the study of the significance of the numerical values of Hebrew letters or concepts. In Hebrew, every letter is also a number. This means that every word or concept will have a numerical value. When we see that two words, groups of words, concepts with even radically different meanings have the same gematria, we are prompted to look for their underlying relationship. There must be such a relationship, or else they would not have the same numerical value.
>
> All that we see with our eyes is the physical manifestation. We see the physical table, but not the spiritual table that makes the physical table possible. The physical table's underlying, unseen reality is that its physicality is being manifested through the letters of the Torah.
>
> Just as the chemical makeup of the entire physical creation runs throughout all matter, and similar chemicals will be found even in objects that appear totally different, so does gematria reflect spiritual relationships between concepts that otherwise would seem totally different.[25]

---

in the Hebrew Alphabet; Waton, *The Key to the Bible*; Wisnefsky, *Apples from the Orchard*.

25. Locks, "Gematria," Mystical Paths.

Table 1. Six Examples of *Gematria*

Letter	Absolute value/ Standard value (*Peshat*), (*Mispar Ragil*), or (*Mispar Hekrehi*)	Ordinal value (*Mispar Sidduri*)	Reduced value (*Mispar Katan*)	*Milium*	*Atbash* (אתבש) aleph tav-bet shin	Ordinal Numerical value of the names of the letters via *Miluim*
א	1 or 1000	1	1	אלף = *aleph* (1) + *lamed* (30) + *pe* (80) = 111	ת = 400	אלף= *aleph* (1) + *lamed* (12) + *pe* (17) = 30
ב	2	2	2	בית= *bet* (2) + *yod* (10) + *tav* (400) = 412	ש = 300	בית = *bet* (2) + *yod* (10) + *tav* (22) = 34
ג	3	3	3	גמל = *gimel* (3) + *mem* (40) + *lamed* (30) = = 73	ר = 200	גמל= *gimel* (3) + *mem* (13) + *lamed* (12) = 28
ד	4	4	4	דלת = *dalet* (4) + *lamed* (30) + *tav* (400) = 434	פ = 100	דלת = *dalet* (4) + *lamed* (12) + *tav* (22) = 38
ה	5	5	5	הא= *he* (5) + *aleph* (1) = 6	צ = 90	הא= *he* (5) + *aleph* (1) = 6
ו	6	6	6	ואו = *vav* (6) + *aleph* (1) + *vav* (6) = 13	פ = 80	ואו = *vav* (6) + *aleph* (1) + *vav* (6) = 13

ז	7	7	7	זין = zayin (7) + yod (10) + nun (50) = 67	ע = 70	זין = zayin (7) + yod (10) + nun (14) = 31
ח	8	8	8	חת = khet (8) + tav (400) = 408	ס = 60	חת = khet (8) + tav (22) = 30
ט	9	9	9	טת = tet (9) + tav (400) = 409	נ = 50	טת = tet (9) + tav (22) = 31
י	10	10	1	יוד = yod (10) + vav (6) + dalet (4) = 20	מ = 40	יוד = yod (10) + vav (6) + dalet (4) = 20
כ , ך	20	11	2	כף = kaph (20) + pe (80) = 100	ל = 30	כף = kaph (11) + pe (17) = 28
ל	30	12	3	למד = lamed (30) + mem (40) + dalet (4) 74	כ = 20	למד = lamed (12) + mem (13) + dalet (4) = 29
מ , ם	40	13	4	מם= mem (40) + mem (40) = 80	י = 10	מם = mem (13) + mem (13) = 26
נ , ן	50	14	5	נון = nun (50) + vav (6) + nun (50) 106	ט= 9	נון = nun (14) + vav (6) + nun (14) = 34

ס	60	15	6	סמך = *samek* (60) + *mem* (40) + *kaph* (20) = 120	8 =ח	סמך = *samek* 15) + *mem* (13) + *kaph* (11) = 39
ע	70	16	7	עין= *ayin* (70) + *yod* (10) + *nun* (50) = 130	7 = ז	עין= *ayin* (16) + *yod* (10) + *nun* (14) = 40
פ , ף	80	17	8	פי = *pe* (80) + *yod* (10) = 90	6 = ו	פי= *pe* (17) + *yod* (10) = 27
צ , ץ	90	18	9	צדי= *tsade* (90) + *dalet* (4) + *yod* (10) = 104	5 = ה	צדי = *tsade* (18) + *dalet* (4) + *yod* (10) = 32
ק	100	19	1	קוף = *qoph* (100) + *vav* (6) + *pe* (80) 186	4 = ד	קוף= *qoph* (19) + *vav* (6) + *qoph* (19) = 44
ר	200	20	2	ריש = *resh* (200) + *yod* (10) + *shin* (300) = 510	3 = ג	ריש= *resh* (20) + *yod* (10) + *shin* (21) = 51
ש	300	21	3	שין = *shin* (300) + *yod* (10) + *nun* (50) = 360	2 = ב	שין = *shin* (21) + *yod* (10) + *nun* (14) = 45
ת	400	22	4	תיו = *tav* (400) + *yod* (10) + *vav* (6) = 416	1=א	תיו = *tav* (22) + *yod* (10) + *vav* (6) = 38

ך	500	23	5				
ם	600	24	6				
ן	700	25	7				
ף	800	26	8				
ץ	900	27	9				

Table 2. Seven Examples of *Gematria* for the Word Israel

	Absolute value/ Standard value (*Peshat*) (*Mispar Ragil*)	Ordinal value (*Mispar Sidduri*)	Reduced value (*Mispar Katan*)	Miluim (Filling) (*Mispar Shemi* or *Millui*)	*At-Bash* (אתבש) *aleph tav—bet shin*	Absolute Value plus the number of letters in the word (*Mispar Musaph*)	Absolute Value plus the number of one for the word itself *Mispari Misafi*)
י	10	1	1	20	40	10	10
ש	300	21	3	360	2	300	300
ר	200	23	2	510	3	200	200
א	1	1	1	111	400	1	1
ל	30	12	3	74	20	30	30
Total	541	58	10 or 1	1075	465	541 + 5 = 546	541 + 1 = 542

Another method of *gematria* we will discuss is the letter expansion of each letter's *milluim* ("filling"). For example, the *millui/milui* of the letter *aleph* is *aleph*. Next, we need to expand the spelling of the three letters that spell out the word *aleph* (see table 3).

Table 3. *Milui* of *Aleph*

א (*aleph*) =	אלף = (*aleph lamed kaph*)
ל (*lamed*) =	למד = (*lamed mem dalet*)
פ (*pe*) =	פה = (*pe he*)

One final method of *gematria* appearing in this book is *Mispar Ha-meruba Haklali*, squaring the letters of the words. That number is followed by *Mispar Katan* (reduced value), dropping the zeroes and adding the digits. (see table 4) Rabbi Eleazar ben Judah of Worms, in *Sefer ha-Hokhmah* (Gate 27: The Gate of Squares), reveals hidden in this technique, within the Torah's first word, *Bereshit* is the name of the Creator: YHVH.

Table 4. The Gate of Squares for *Bereshit*

The Letter Squared	Squaring Its *Gematria*	Numerical Value
bet X *bet* =	2 X 2 =	4
resh X *resh* =	200 X 200 =	40,000
aleph X *aleph* =	1 X 1 =	1
shin X *shin* =	300 X 300 =	90,000
yod X *yod* =	10 X 10 =	100
tav X *tav* =	400 X 400 =	160,000

Thus, 4 + 4 + 1 + 9 + 1 + 1 + 6 = 26.

Also, there were twenty-six generations from Adam to Moses and it also being the *gematria* of YHVH.[26]

1.6. DERASH

ד *Derash* (דרש; *derash* = *dalet resh shin*) is an approach that is concerned with the homiletic or interpretative meaning of a word, phrase, or verse. Therefore, this technique incorporates drawing out teaching or exposition. From the Hebrew *derash*, it means to "seek" or to "search" the non-literal, homiletic interpretation of Scripture (moralistic meaning), as in the midrash or Talmudic haggadot. There are two types:

1. *midrash halakhah*—Scriptural sources for Jewish Laws.

2. *midrash haggadah*—blend of history, legend, and poetry.

1.7. SOD

ס- *Sod* (סוד; *samech vav dalet*) deals with the esoteric, mystical, and super-rational dimensions often illuminated by the teachings found in the Kabbalah. Kabbalah refers to that what was received. Several significant sources are *Sefer Yetzirah*, the *Zohar*, and the *Sefer ha-Bahir*. *Sod* is the highest and most profound level of investigation. It includes concepts such as the Four Worlds (Divine "Garments") and the ten *sefirot* (Divine instruments through which everything came into being).

According to the Kabbalah, there exist four spiritual worlds, and each world corresponds to a means of exegesis:

26. Alter, *Why the Torah Begins*, 246.

1. *Sod—Atzilut* or Emanation

2. *Derash—Beriy'ah* or Creation

3. *Remez—Yetzirah* or Formation

4. *Peshat—Asiyah* or Making

In addition, the Kabbalah discusses the existence of ten *sefirot*. These *sefirot* are like channels of Divine energy or lifeforce. Jacob Immanuel Schochet elaborates that the "Names or attributes apply only to manifestations, to those aspects of Divinity which are revealed in, and to His creation."[27] Ginsburgh writes, "The ten *sefirot* are the stages in the Creative process imprinted on all aspects of reality."[28] *Tiferet* is the central *sefirah* of focus in this text.

Tiferet is the sixth *sefirah*. Significantly, Jacob (who is also Israel) is the personality associated with this *sefirah*. Hence, its obvious importance. *Tiferet* is harmony, truth, compassion, and beauty. It balances the powers of attraction and repulsion (see figure 1). Therefore, its location is in the middle column of the three-column array.

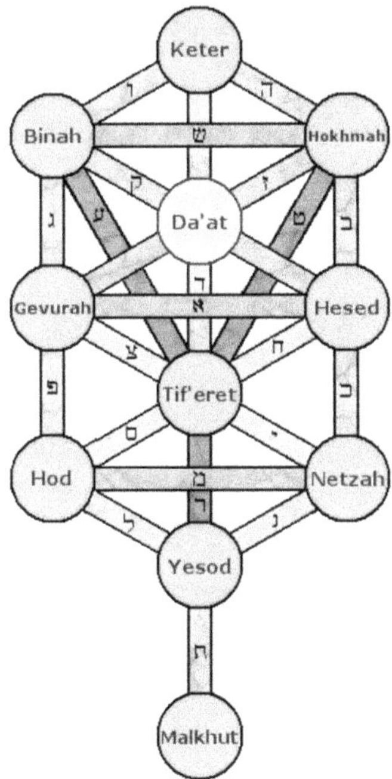

Figure 1: The Ten *Sefirot*

27. Schochet, *Mystical Concepts in Chassidism*, 59–60.

28. Ginsburgh, *The Hebrew Letters*, 355.

The center column is discussed extensively in the Kabbalah. Interestingly, the center column in the three-column array consists of the *sefirot* *Keter* (one), *Tiferet* (six), *Yesod* (nine), and *Malkut* (ten).[29] The summation of the locations is twenty-six, being the *gematria* of the name YHVH.

Rabbi Jacob Immanuel Schochet provides a detailed and comprehensible discussion on the *sefirot*.

> The *Sefirot* are thus Divine emanations, various phases in the manifestation of Divinity. As we speak of them in terms of numerous gradations, extreme care must be taken to avoid any fatal conception of dualism or a plurality in the G-dhead. There is no suggestion whatever that the *Sefirot* are to be taken as entities distinct and separate from the *En Sof*. On the contrary, there is a basic and intrinsic unity between the *En Sof* and the *Sefirot*. This absolute and intrinsic unity has already been stressed in the ancient *Sefer Yetzirah*: "The ten *Sefirot* are without anything (*beli-mah*), Their end is wedged in their beginning, their beginning is wedged in their end—like a flame bound up in the coal. For the Eternal is One, and there is no second to Him, and prior to One what you can count! [*Sefer Yetzirah* 1:7][30]

Readers are strongly encouraged to examine his text and those of other authorities. Additional beneficial materials are standard references (encyclopedia entries) and books devoted to Kabbalah.

---

29. In some configurations *Da'at* (knowledge) appears, although it is not properly a *sefirah*, but rather is all ten *sefirot* united as one.

30. Schochet, *Mystical Concepts in Chassidism*, 62.

2.

Vayishlach

Vayishlach is the eighth weekly *parashah* in the annual cycle of Torah readings. In the Hebrew Bible, often, the number eight alludes to that which transcends physicality. Twice in *Vayishlach* (Genesis 32:4–36:43), the divine origin of the name Israel appears. The significant sections recorded in the narratives are chapter 32, verses 25 through 31, and later in chapter 35, verses 9 through 10.

2.1. OVERVIEW OF GENESIS CHAPTER 32

Jacob returns to the Holy Land, later called the *Eretz Yisrael* or the Land of Israel, after his earlier departure journey and a lengthy stay in Charan. Thirty-four years earlier, he fled to escape Esau, his twin brother's revenge. He stole the blessings from their father, Isaac. Jacob sent messengers to appease his twin brother Esau, yearning for reconciliation. However, his messengers returned with a report that his brother was coming to meet him with 400 armed men. Jacob prepared for war, prayed, and sent Esau a gift of hundreds of livestock to appease him.

That night, Jacob ferried his family and possessions across the ford of the Jabbok. However, Jacob remained behind and encountered "a man" (*ish*). The Sages generally think that this "*ish*" was an angel. Rabbis and scholars dispute the man's identity or even his (its) reality. (See Bereshit Rabbah 77:3)

Conversely, in some traditions, Jacob was the angel Israel who would wrestle the angel, Uriel. Summarizing the literature, Howard Schwartz writes

Jacob was no ordinary man. If the truth be known, his true name was Israel, and he was an angel of God, the very archangel of the power of the Lord and the first minister before the face of God. Indeed, he was the first living being to whom God gave life, with the beauty of Adam . . .

When the angel Israel descended to earth and became Jacob, he forgot his divine origin. God tried to remind him when He sent him the dream of the ladder reaching from earth to heaven, so that he might glimpse the celestial world he had left behind. In the dream angels of God were ascending and descending on it (Genesis 28:12). For the angels who had accompanied him from his father's house went up to heaven to announce to the angels on high: "Come and see Jacob the pious, whose image is fixed upon the Throne of Glory, the one you have longed to see." Then the rest of the holy angels of the Lord came down to look at him. That is why the angels went up and down the ladder, for they ascended to see the face carved on the celestial throne, and they descended to see the face of Jacob as he slept, whose features were identical to those carved on high . . .

Thus when Jacob wrestled with the angel at the River Yabbok, the struggle was not that of a man and angel, but that of two angels—Uriel and Israel. Some say that Uriel had been sent to remind Jacob of his divine origin, saying, "Know that you were once an angel, who descended to earth and took up dwelling among humans and your name became Jacob. *Now your name shall no longer be called Jacob, but Israel*" (Genesis 32:29). Others say that Uriel wrestled with Jacob, saying, "My name will take precedence over your name and the names of every other angel." At first Jacob did not understand, but suddenly he remembered that he once was an angel. And Jacob said, "Are you not Uriel? Have you forgotten that I am Israel, the chief commander among the heavenly hosts?" And Jacob called out God's secret Name and thus defeated him.[1]

The *Prayer of Joseph* is a pseudepigraphic source (a text whose claimed authorship is unfounded) of the Hebrew Bible. It was composed either in Aramaic (if Jewish) or Greek (if Christian) in the 1st century CE. The text is almost lost, and only a few fragments have survived. The angel's identification as Uriel, with whom Jacob wrestles, derives from the *Prayer of Joseph* 1:5–9.

---

1. Schwartz, *Tree of Souls*, #470.

The *Prayer of Joseph* was well known in the early 3rd century by Origen of Alexandria. He was an early Christian scholar, ascetic, and theologian. He points out that the text was in use among the Jewish people.

Only three fragments have survived. Fragment A is the longest. The surviving extract is from Origen's *"Commentary on the Gospel of John"*—Book 2.31(25), 186–192. The text of Fragment A follows:

> Thus Jacob says: "I, Jacob, who speak to you, and Israel, I am an angel of God, a ruling spirit, and Abraham and Isaac were created before every work of God; and I am Jacob, called Jacob by men, but my name is Israel, called Israel by God, a man seeing God, because I am the first-born of every creature which God caused to live." And he adds: "When I was coming from Mesopotamia of Syria, Uriel, the angel of God, came forth, and said, I have come down to the earth and made my dwelling among men, and I am called Jacob by name. He was angry with me and fought with me and wrestled against me, saying that his name and the name of Him who is before every angel should be before my name. And I told him his name and how great he was among the sons of God; Are you not Uriel my eighth, and I am Israel and archangel of the power of the Lord and a chief captain among the sons of God? Am not I Israel, the first minister in the sight of God, and I invoked my God by the inextinguishable name?
>
> Are you not Uriel my eighth, and I am Israel and archangel of the power of the Lord and a chief captain among the sons of God? Am not I Israel, the first minister in the sight of God, and I invoked my God by the inextinguishable name?"[2]

Returning to the Torah text, during Jacob's encounter, he wrestles until daybreak. Through that encounter, Jacob suffers a dislocated hip. Nonetheless, he defeats his opponent. At this time, his adversary bestows a prediction that he will receive the name Israel. In addition, the angel explains the rationale behind that new name: *"Your name shall no longer be Jacob, but Israel; for you have contended with God and with men, and have prevailed."* (NASB) [*or "beings divine and human," NJPS*]

2.2. THE SIGNIFICANT TEXT OF CHAPTER 32

> *25 When the man saw that he had not prevailed against him, he touched the socket of Jacob's hip; and the socket of Jacob's hip was dislocated while he wrestled with him. 26 Then he said, "Let me*

2. Quoted in Origin, *Commentary on the Gospel of John—Book II*, 25.

go, for the dawn is breaking." But he said, "I will not let you go unless you bless me." 27 So he said to him, "What is your name?" And he said, "Jacob." 28 Then he said, "Your name shall no longer be Jacob, but Israel; for you have contended with God and with men, and have prevailed." 29 And Jacob asked him and said, "Please tell me your name." But he said, "Why is it that you ask my name?" And he blessed him there. 30 So Jacob named the place Peniel, for he said, "I have seen God face to face, yet my life has been spared. (NASB)

2.3. OVERVIEW OF GENESIS 35:9–10

Shortly after Jacob encountered "the man," he arrived in Bethel. Here, God appeared to Jacob and informed him, *"You shall be called Jacob no more."* Instead, he is to be called Israel. Significantly, the Torah emphatically concludes: *"And He"* — God — *"called his name Israel."* There is no explanation for the changed name. Nor is there any mention of his wrestling match with a man (possible angel).

In the Tanakh, name changes are in noteworthy personalities. Unlike four individuals, Jacob does not receive an extra letter to his birth name. Those four individuals who received an extra letter for their names were:

1. Joshua received a *yod*,

2. Abraham received a *he*,

3. Jethro received a *vav*, and[3]

4. Sarah received a *he*

When combined these four letters spell YHVH—the Tetragrammaton.

2.4 THE SIGNIFICANT TEXT OF CHAPTER 35

9 Then God appeared to Jacob again when he came from Paddan-aram, and He blessed him. 10 God said to him, "Your name is Jacob; You shall no longer be called Jacob, But Israel shall be your name." So He called him Israel. (NASB)

---

3. Rashi on Exodus 18:1.

3.

A *Peshat* Analysis of Israel

(1) Philo of Alexandria (ca. 20 BCE—ca. 50 CE)

Why Certain Names in the Holy Scriptures are Changed

XII. (81) But it has also happened that Jacob had his name changed to Israel; and this, too, was a felicitous alteration. Why so? Because the name Jacob means "a supplanter," but the name Israel signifies "the man who sees God." Now it is the employment of a supplanter, who practices virtue, to move, and disturb, and upset the foundations of passion on which it is established, and whatever there is of any strength which is founded on them. But these things are not brought about without a struggle or without severe labour; but only when any one, having gone through all the labours of prudence, then proceeds to practise himself in the exercises of the soul and to wrestle against the reasonings which are hostile to it, and which seek to torment it; but it is the part of him who sees God not to depart from the sacred contest without the crown of victory, but rather to carry off the prize of triumph. (82) And what more flourishing and more suitable crown could be woven for the victorious soul than one by which it will be able acutely and clearly to behold the living God? At least a beautiful prize is thus proposed for the soul which delights in the practice of virtue, namely, the being endowed with sight adequate to the clear comprehension of the only thing which is really worth beholding.[1]

1. Philo, "*Why Certain Names,*" 253–54.

(2) Philo of Alexandria (ca. 20 BCE—ca. 50 CE)

> Book 1 *On Dreams* [A Treatise on the Doctrine that Dreams Are Sent from God] XXVII. (1.170–172)]
>
> (1.170) So that it is thus very natural for Abraham, as one who had been improved by instruction, to be called the father of Jacob, who arrived at his height by practice. By which expression is indicated that not so much the relationship of one man to the other, but that the power which is fond of hearing is very ready for learning; the power which is devoted to practice being also well suited for wrestling. (1.171) If, however, this practiser of virtue runs on vigorously towards the end and learns to see clearly what he previously only dreamed of in an indistinct way, being altered and re-stamped with a better character, and being called Israel, that is, "the man who sees God," instead of Jacob, that is, "supplanter," he then is no longer set down as the son of Abraham, as his father, of him who derived wisdom from instructions, but as the son of Israel, who was born excellent by nature. (1.172)
>
> These statements are not fables of my own invention, but are the oracle written on the sacred pillars. For, says the scripture: *"Israel having departed, he and all that had come to the well of the oath, and there he sacrificed a sacrifice to the God of his father Isaac."* {41} {#ge 46:1.} Do you not now perceive that this present assertion has reference not to the relationship between mortal men, but, as was said before, to the nature of things? For look at what is before us. At one time, Jacob is spoken of as the son of Abraham, and at another time he is called Israel, the son of Isaac on account of the reason which we have thus accurately investigated.[2]

Philo uses to interpret *Israel* as ὁρῶν θεόν, "(the one) who sees God." By doing so, he probably reproduces an interpretation of the Hebrew name *Israel* as a contraction of *ish roê el,* "the man (someone) who sees God."[3]

> To Philo, "seeing" God is the philosopher's goal. Since he explains that "Israel" means "one who sees God," "Israel" can represent those who achieve this goal. "Israel," however, is also the name of the Biblical patriarch and nation and their Jewish descendants whom God chose to participate in His covenant.

2. Philo, "A Treatise on the Doctrine that Dreams, 327–28.

3. Birnbaum, *The Place of Judaism,* 70–72.

This study, then, focuses upon how Philo understands the relationship between "Israel" and the Jews.[4]

(3) Philo of Alexandria (ca. 20 BCE—ca. 50 CE)

Questions and Answers on Genesis 4

#233 (Genesis 27. 39)

Why, after Esau cried aloud and wept, did his father begin to bless him?

For he saw him weeping and shedding tears, and he believed, as was natural, that he was groaning and lamenting and bewailing his own unhappy life, and his indecent ways. Similar to this was the way in which (God) had pity on those whose souls were afflicted in Egypt—namely, those of) Israel, a name (meaning) "one who sees."[i]

[i] The etymology of the name "Israel" as "one who sees (god) is frequently given by Philo, but the syntax and meaning of this sentence are far from clear.[5]

(4) Josephus (37–ca. 100)

Antiquities of the Jews (Chapter XX Concerning the Meeting of Jacob and Esau)

When Jacob had made these appointments all the day, and night came on, he moved on with his company; and as they were gone over a certain river called Jabboc, Jacob was left behind; and meeting with an angel, he wrestled with him, the angel beginning the struggle; but he prevailed over the angel, who used a voice, and spake to him in words, exhorting him to be pleased with what had happened to him, and not to suppose that his victory was a small one, but that he had overcome a divine angel, and to esteem the victory as a sign of great blessings that should come to him; and that his offspring should never fail; and that no man should be too hard for his power. He also commanded him to be called Israel, which in the Hebrew tongue signifies *one that struggled with the divine angel.**

* [The translator comments] In the meantime, it is certain that the Hellenists of the first century, in Egypt and elsewhere,

---

4. Birnbaum, *The Place of Judaism*, 70–72; Also see Hayward, "Philo, the Septuagint of Genesis," 32:24–32, 209–26.

5. Philo, *Supplement 1 Questions and Answers*, 532.

interpreted *Israel* to be *a man seeing God* as is evident from the argument fore cited.[6]

(5) Mekhilta de-Rabbi Shimon bar Yohai (ca. 220–500 CE)

XLIX:I, 4–5

"*Thus shall you say to the House of Jacob*" (Exod. 19:3)—All is in the merit of Ya'akov. "*And tell the children of Israel*" (Exod. 19:3)—Everything is in the merit of Israel. Another interpretation: "*Thus shall you say to the House of Jacob*" (Exod. 19:3) —Jacob was given the name Ya'akov originally, but now has merited to attain the exalted name, *Israel, for he wrestled with God and prevailed* (Gen. 32:29).[7]

(6) The Talmud (ca. 450–550 CE)

Hullin 92a (cf. Berakhot 12b and 13a)

The verse states: "*And he said: Your name shall no longer be called Jacob, but Israel; for you have striven with angels [elohim] and with men, and have prevailed.*"[8]

(7) Genesis Rabbah (ca. 500 CE)

Vayyishlach 78.3

FOR THOU HAST STRIVEN WITH ELOHIM[3] AND WITH MEN, AND HAST PREVAILED (XXXII, 29): thou hast striven with celestial beings and conquered them, and with mortals, and hast conquered them. 'With celestial beings' alludes to the angel. R. Ham b. Hanina said: It was Esau's guardian angel. That was what Jacob meant when he said to him: *Forasmuch as I have seen thy face, as one seeth the face of Elohim (ib.* XXXIII, 10): even as the face of God denotes judgement' even as with respect to the face of God [it is written], *And none shall appear before My face empty-handed* [Ex. XXIII, 15], so art thou; none may appear before thy face empty-handed. 'With mortals, and hast conquered them'—by that, Esau and his chiefs are meant.

6. Josephus, *Josephus Complete Works*, 43.

7. *Mekhilta de-Rabbi Shimon bar Yohai*, 49:1

8. *Koren Talmud Bavli, Vol 37: Hullin Part 1, English.*

Another interpretation of FOR THOU HAST STRIVEN
(SARITHA) WITH GOD: it is thou whose features are engraven
on high.

[3] E.V. 'God', but the Midrash translates angels, celestial beings, as
is justified by the context.[9]

(8) Rabbi Shlomo Yitzchak (Rashi) (ca. 1075– ca. 1105)

Genesis 32, 29

[THY NAME SHALL] *NO MORE BE CALLED JACOB* [*BUT
ISRAEL*] (literally, "not Jacob — supplanting — shall any more
be said to thee") — It shall no longer be said that the blessings
came to you through supplanting and subtlety but through
noble conduct (שררה) and in an open manner. Because later on
the Holy One, blessed be He, will reveal Himself to you at Bethel
and will change your name. There He will bless you, and I shall
be there and admit your right to them (the blessings). It is to this
that the passage refers (Hosea 12:5), "*And he strove with an angel
and prevailed; he wept and made supplication unto him*" — it
means the angel wept and made supplication unto him (Jacob).
What was the subject of his supplication? This is stated in the
next verse: *At Bethel He will meet us and there He will speak with
us — implying the request.* "Wait until he will speak with us there,
and then I will admit your right to the blessings."[10]

35, 10

THY NAME SHALL NOT BE CALLED ANY MORE JACOB—
which means a man who comes as a lurker and trickster, but it
shall be Israel (ישראל), which signifies Prince and Chief.[11]

(9) Rabbi Samuel ben Meir ("Rashbam") (1085–1158)

Commentary on the Torah
The word is derived from *ShRH* in Hosea 12:4, . . . "*and with his
might he fought with a Divine being* (reference to Yaakov)."[12]

9. Freedman, *Midrash Rabbah: Genesis*, 2:717–18.
10. Rashi, *Pentateuch with Rashi's Commentary*.
11. Rashi, *Pentateuch with Rashi's Commentary*.
12. Samuel ben Meir, *Mikraot Gedolot*, 642.

(10) Rabbi David Kimchi ("RaDaK") (1160–1235)

Torah Commentary

32:29 . . . the name Yisrael denotes the nation founded by "Yaakov" . . .

The reason for the name change was revealed by the angel.

. . . with angel. He wrestled with you and could not overpower you to the extent of felling you.[13]

(11) Rabbi Moses ben Nahman—Nachmanides (the Ramban) (1194–1270)

Commentary on the Torah

10. *THY NAME IS JACOB.* God is saying, "Now you are still called Jacob even though the lord of Esau has changed your name because he was sent to you to change your name. However, *from now on, thy name shall not be called any more Jacob, but Israel shall be thy name,*" this being the meaning of the end of the verse, *and He called his name Israel.* It may be that it alludes to the fact that He called his name Israel in addition to the name Jacob, but not that it be forbidden for him to be called Jacob.[14]

(12) Menachem ben Binyamin Recanati (c. 1223–1290)

Perush 'Al ha-Torah

And he said, Yea, Jacob shall no more say thy name, but Israel; for thou hast *Sarit* [= struggled or prevailed] with God, and with men, and hast been able to overcome. You will find the change of name in Abraham and Jacob and not in Isaac because his religion is law and does not pass first as grace and mercy.[15]

13. Kimchi, *Mikraot Gedolot*, 648–49.

14. Nachmanides, *Commentary on the Torah: Genesis*, 424–25.

15. Recanati, *Perush 'Al ha-Torah*. Note: Abraham is associated with the attribute of *chesed* (giving, kindness, and love), whereas Isaac is associated with the quality of *gevurah* (discipline, restraint, severity, and justice). In contrast, Jacob/Israel is linked with the attribute and *sefirah* of *Tiferet*, the quality of harmony and truth. Therefore, Israel is a blending of (opposites) his father and grandfather.

(13) Hezekiah ben Manoah or Chizkuni (1250–1310)

Chizkuni Torah Commentary

Genesis 35:10 *"your name has been Yaakov; it will no longer be Yaakov;"* The Torah means that henceforth his name would no longer <u>only</u> be "Yaakov," but the name "Yisrael" would be added to it. If the name "Yaakov" were to be eliminated completely, this would be interpreted as having been a name describing a person with negative character traits up to now. (Compare Esau's comment in Genesis 27,36) Henceforth the Torah will refer to Yaakov-Yisrael sometimes by his original name and sometimes only by his additional name. When G-d changed Avram's name to Avraham, He had *never* said that שמך אברם, [*shimecha Avram*] "your name is or was Avram." This is why the sages have said that anyone referring to Avraham as Avram, is equivalent to violating a positive commandment of the Torah (Talmud *Berachot* 13).

כי אם ישראל יהיה שמך, *"but your name shall be Yisrael."* The name implies that the one possessing it wields authority, as the angel had said to Yaakov: *"you have contended with Divinity and you have prevailed."* (32,29) The name is very appropriate for you as you will be the founding father of kings. Rashi here claims that the reference in this verse is to King Sha-ul and his son *Ish Boshet*.

Should you ask that we have been taught (in *Sanhedrin* 20) that Avner was punished for having delayed David's occupying the throne of the Kingdom for two and a half years, i.e., the years during which *Ish Boshet* ruled after he appointed him as Sha-ul's successor; why would he be punished for this, seeing it has been decreed already in the Torah that he would rule (according to Rashi)? We would have to answer that he was not punished for having crowned *Ish Boshet*, but because he had crowned *Ish Boshet* not because he considered him as fit to rule, but that he was motivated exclusively by trying to thwart David from ascending the throne.[16]

(14) Rabbi Bahya ben Asher (1255–1340)

Midrash Rabbeinu Bachya Torah Commentary

Genesis 32:29 *"for you have contended with Divine forces."* In this instance the word *elohim* refers to the angel representing Esau with whom Yaakov had wrestled. The word *ve-im anashim,*

---

16. Chizkuni, *Torah Commentary*, 258.

in the same line, refer to Lavan and Esau. According to *Bereshit Rabbah* 78, 3, the words . . . mean that Yaakov's countenance was engraved on the throne of G'd and the angel had realized this after looking at Yaakov.

35:10 שמך יעקב [*shimecha Yaakov*] *"your name Yaakov, etc."* According to Nachmanides, although Esau's guardian angel had already told Yaakov that his name would henceforth be Israel, (32,29) G'd told him that as of this moment his name was still Yaakov. However, from that time on his name would be Israel. This is the meaning of the words: ויקרי שמו ישראל. [*Vayikra Shemo Yisrael* = *"Listen to Me, O Jacob, Israel"*] Thus far Nachmanides' comment. This then is the meaning of Isaiah 48,12 וישראל מקוראי , [*v'Yisrael m'qoraiy*] *"and Israel whom I have called."*

Rabbeinu Chananel explains that the name Israel which G'd bestowed on Yaakov was in addition to the name Yaakov which Yaakov retained. The word עוד in our verse means "only, exclusively." The correct translation of our verse is: "your name will no longer be Yaakov exclusively, but your name will (also) be Israel." We find something analogous to this in Jeremiah 3, 16 לא יאמרו עוד ארון ברית ה' *"they will no longer refer to the ark of G'd as the only location where G'd can be found, etc."* but the *whole of Jerusalem will be so designated."* They will refer to the whole of Jerusalem as כסא ה' *"the throne of the Lord."* Similarly, here; the words כא אם ישראל יהיה שמך *"but Israel shall be your name, i.e., sometimes you will be referred to as "Yaakov," other times as "Israel."* This is precisely what the prophet had in mind in Isaiah [48:12] . . .

We find something similar in Isaiah 46,28 *"do not fear My servant Yaakov, do not be scared Israel."*[17]

(15) Rabbi Jacob ben Asher (R'osh) (ca. 1269– ca. 1343)

Tur on the Torah

35, 10 *"your name is Yaakov."* Your name is still Yaakov even though the celestial representative of Esau had changed it to "Yisrael," it had not been that angel's mission to change your name. However, from now on your name will be Yisrael. The meaning of the apparent repetition, "He called his name 'Yisrael' is that this was an additional name and it was not forbidden to call him Yaakov.[18]

17. Asher, *Torah Commentary*, 2:509, 530–31.

18. Asher, *Tur on the Torah,* 285.

(16) Rabbi Ovadiah ben Jacob Sforno (ca. 1500—ca. 1550)

Commentary on the Torah
32:29 . . . The reason for the name change was revealed by the angel.

. . . with angel. He wrestled with you and could not overpower you to the extent of felling you.

35:10 seeing that you will rule, תשתרר over the remnants of all the nations that have ceased to exist as such. This also corresponds to the previous prophecy of Bilaam in Numbers 24, 17 . . . *"he (Yaakov) will smash all the foundation of the sons of Seth* (mankind.)"

He blessed him in that the predictions which were meant for the end of time, were beginning to be implemented already from that time on, and not only while Yaakov was on holy soil in the land of Canaan, but even when he would be outside (as in Egypt). From this time on no one who would attack Yaakov and his family would meet with success. This was the meaning of what our sages said in *Sanhedrin* 76 that "wherever Yaakov and his family walked on they became princes over their masters," and this is what the prophet Jeremiah bewailed in Lamentations 1, 1 as what the Jewish people lost as a result of the destruction of the Temple.[19]

(17) Rabbi Ashkenazi Jacob ben Isaac [Yaakov ben Yitzchak Ashkenazi] (1550–1628)

Tzeénah Ureénah: "Go Ye and See": A Rabbinical Commentary on Genesis
[35]9, 10 *And God blessed him*, and condoled with him in his mourning, and said, "Thy name shall not be called *Jacob*, which means *Falsehood*, that thou hast taken the blessing with falsehood but *Israel* shall be thy name, which means *a Prince*." The B'chai and the Chizkûni say: Thy name shall not be Jacob only, but at times shalt also be called Israel; thou shalt have both names.[20]

19. Sforno, *Mikraot Gedolot*, 653, 680–81.
20. Yaakov ben Yitzchak Ashkenazi, *Tzeénah Ureénah*, 212.

(18) Rabbi Levi Yitzchok of Berditchev (1740–1809)

Kedushat Levi Torah Commentary

"He said: *'your name will no longer be Yaakov, but Israel, for you have contended both with celestial forces and with human forces and you have prevailed.'*" There are people who constantly remain attached to G'd even while they are engaged in conversation with human beings. There are other people, who while engaged in a conscious effort to serve the Lord, concentrate on this to the exclusion of everything else; whereas while they are engaged in mundane activities such as business conversations with their peers, they cannot at the same time remain conscious of their duties towards their Creator. The first type of person deserves the title: "Israel:" as the letters רשר, "upright," as well as the letters ראש, "head," are part of that title. The second category of person, (observant Jew) is called יעקב , i.e., עקב-' that his attachment to G'd is עקב [*'akev = ayin kaf bet*], "secondary," just as a heel is a secondary and not a primary organ. Esau's celestial representative acknowledged that Yaakov was a person of the first category since in his dealings with man he never lost sight of his primary duties to his G'd.[21]

(19) Rabbi Meir Leibush Jehiel Michael Malbim (1809–1879)

Malbim Commentary on the Torah

His blessing was that no more shall his name be called Yaqov but Yisrael, for he had triumphed with the power of his essential self and his inner soul. Hence, *for you have contended with angels and with men.* This is within you the godly power that derives from the soul, which is a godly portion from On-high, and the human power that derives from the physical-material—the voice of Yaqov and the hands of Esav—and with them have you won this battle.[22]

21. Levi Yitzchok of Bereditchev, *Kedushat Levi Torah,* 200.

22. Malbim, *Malbim Commentary on the Torah,* 3:100–101.

(20) Rabbi Samson Raphael Hirsch (1808–1888)

The Pentateuch. Volume 1. *Genesis*

V. 29. thy name shall no longer have the meaning, be explained as "the one who is destined to hold on to the heel." Not, it shall no longer be called (he only received the name Israel later on, from God, Ch. XXXV, 10), but the name Jacob itself shall be understood as Israel. ישראל: (from שרה [*sin resh he*], one of the aspects of ruling, that of being superior, greater) means literally, God is the All-conquering One. Who is superior to everything else in Power and Greatness, and here the angel, (the genius of Esau I.L.) declares that in truth is to be what the meaning of the condition, which is expressed by יעקב [Yaakov]. Only when a יעקב [Yaakov], one who, to all outward appearances is under the heel of all others, obtains the victory over the most vicious attacks of enemies fully equipped with all material means, does this victory show the existence of a spiritual power which outweighs all material might and power. It shows the existence of an Almighty God, Who reveals Himself just in the victorious endurance of this outwardly weak opponent, so that יעקב [Yaakov] is just therein to be regarded and understood as ישראל [Yisrael].[23]

(21) Rabbi Menachem M. Kasher (1895–1983)

Encyclopedia of Biblical Interpretation Commentary:

[29] *no more Jacob. a.* You will no longer be known by the name Jacob only, but will receive an additional name, Israel. *b.* The new appellation will be regarded as your principal name. *c.* The angel did not himself bestow the additional name but merely foretold that God was going to bestow it. *d.* In the Messianic time, however, the name Jacob will be given up entirely and only Israel will remain. *Jacob.* That is, "the Supplanter," prevailing over opponents by deceit. Israel. The name is clearly a title of victory; probably "a champion of God." striven. *a.* Or, thou art to be regarded as a prince: on a par with angels. *b.* Render, didst prevail. *With God.* I.e., with an angel of God.[24]

---

23. Hirsch, *The Pentateuch*, 1:506.
24. Kasher, *Encyclopedia of Biblical Interpretation*, 4:155.

(22) Rabbi Gunter Plaut (1912–2012)

The Torah: A Modern Commentary

This tradition is not aware of Jacob's wrestling bout with the angel . . . nor of the site having been named El-bethel. Traditional explanations: God confers what His angel has done "in the heat of the contest."[25]

(23) Eliyahu Munk (ca. 1922–)

The Just Lives by His Faith

Yaakov-Yisrael

Yaakov now realizes that the stranger was more than an ordinary human being. He demands that the angel reveal his name. This the angel refuses to do but he does agree to bless Yaakov, assuring him that he had overcome a divine force and that the name Yaakov which had always carried a stigma with it was a misnomer and that he should rightfully be called Yisrael, someone who had contended with Divine forces and had prevailed.[26]

(24) Nahum M. Sarna (1923–2005)

The JPS Torah Commentary: Genesis

32: 29 The innovation of the name "Israel" in the Bible is associated with struggle and triumph in the face of overwhelming odds. Curiously and instructively, the earliest extrabiblical document to mention Israel, the victory hymn of King Merneptah of Egypt (ca. 1206 BCE), reports that "Israel is laid waste, his seed is not," while the second, the victory inscription of King Mesha of Moab (ca. 830 BCE), declares "Israel has perished forever."[27]

35:9–10 Jacob's name is changed to Israel for the second time. In 32:28–29 it was not God personally but an angelic being, most likely the celestial patron of Esau, who made the pronouncement. Moreover, it was made on the other side of the Jordan. Therefore, the new name "Israel" needs to be confirmed and validated by God Himself in the promised land. The fact that God is said to

25. Plaut, *The Torah: A Modern*, 233.
26. Munk, *The Just Lives by His Faith*, 167.
27. Sarna, *The JPS Torah Commentary: Genesis*, 227.

appear "again" and that, remarkably, no rationale for the new name is given here, shows a dependency on the earlier narrative.

The significance of the new name emerges from the succeeding blessing, which is national in scope and consists of the promise of fertility, nationhood, kingship, and territory. Jacob, by becoming also Israel, is the true heir to the Abrahamic promises, the one through whom the nation of Israel is to come into being.[28]

(25) Robert Alter (1935–)

Introductory remark. Alter connects three subjects discussed throughout this text—the etymology of the name Israel, the *'el* ending, and the verb *sarah*. A list of names ending with *'el* is in appendixes 3 and 4.

> *The Five Books of Moses: A Translation with Commentary*
>
> In any case, he [Jacob's adversary] etymologizes the name *Yisra'el* as "he strives with God." In fact, names with the 'el ending generally make God the subject, not the object, of the verb in the name. This particular verb, *sarah*, is a rare one, and there is some question about its meaning, though an educated guess about the original sense of the name would be: 'God will rule,' or perhaps, 'God will prevail.'[29]

(26) Yair Zakovitch (1945–)

> *Jacob: Unexpected Patriarch*
>
> The name change, denoting a change in destiny, continues the patriarchal tradition that began with the change from Abram to Abraham (Genesis 17:5) and Sarai to Sarah (vv 15–16). In our story, the root *'-k-b* (*ya'aqov*) is exchanged for *s-r-b* (*sa-rita*) In order to account for the ultimate syllable in the name *yisra'el*, the text admits that Jacob wrestled *with God* (*'im 'elohim*): Jacob is the one who "strove with God"![30]

---

28. Sarna, *The JPS Torah Commentary: Genesis*, 241–42.

29. Alter, *The Five Books of Moses*, 181. Comment: Robert Alter (no relation to this author) is an American professor of Hebrew and comparative literature at the University of California, Berkeley. He has taught there since 1967. Over two decades, he wrote this translation and commentary. Published by W.W. Norton, it has been widely acclaimed and won the PEN Center Literary Award for Translation.

30 Zakovitch, *Jacob Unexpected Patriarch*, 102.

(27) Everett Fox (1947–)

The Five Books of Moses
29. *God-Fighter*: The name may actually mean "God fights." Buber further conjectured that it means "God rules," containing the kernel of ancient Israel's concept of itself, but he retained "Fighter of God" in the translation.[31]

(28) Rabbi Menachem Leibtag (1954–)

"Yaakov's Name Change to Yisrael"
Although wounded and limping, Yaakov emerges victorious from this confrontation, thus earning his new name: "*Your name shall no longer be Yaakov, but Yisrael, for you have **fought** with beings divine ('Elokim') and human ('anashim') and **triumphed**"* (32:29).

Thus, the name Yisrael may reflect the character of one triumphant in battle. Yaakov's new name is significant for it reflects his capability to engage head on in battle. In order to become a nation, this trait—represented by the name 'Yisrael'—is crucial.[32]

(29) Rabbi Rachel Barenblat (the Velveteen Rabbi) (1975–)

"Seeing the wrestle as a blessing: thoughts on Vayishlach"
My teacher and friend Rabbi Arthur Waskow translates Israel as God-wrestler. Israel is the one who wrestles with God. And as we are the people Israel, the community which bears his name, then wrestling with God is our task, too. Perhaps this means wrestling with the texts in Torah which challenge us, or wrestling with ethical questions about what kind of life we intend to lead.[33]

(30) Rabbi Tzemah Yoreh (1986–)

"Jacob is named Israel (Twice): Why does the name of Jacob remain?"

31. Fox, *The Five Books of Moses*, 155.
32. Leibtag, "Yaakov's Name Change to Yisrael."
33. Barenblat, "Seeing the wrestle as a blessing."

The new name ישראל "Israel" is a combination of the verb ש.ר.ה.
[*sin resh he*), "to strive with," and a designation for God, אל [*el*
spelled *aleph lamed*]. The passage uniquely describes a person
successfully battling God or his messenger, a suitable folk etymology for the origin of Israel's name.[34]

(31) bible.ort.org

You have become great . . .

(*Targum*). Or, 'You have become a prince (*sar*) among the angels
and man' (Ralbag). Others have, 'You have fought (or struggled)
with a divine being and you have won' (Bereshit Rabbah; Josephus 1:2:2; Septuagint; cf. Hosea 4:5). The root of the word
sari-tha here is thus *sarah*, meaning to contend or 'fight to win'
(Radak, *Sherashim*. cf. Hosea 9:6). It is related to the root *sarar*,
to rule; cf. Numbers 16:13, Esther 1:22, Proverbs 8:16. Also see
Judges 9:22, Hosea 8:4. Israel (*Yisrael*) thus means, 'he who will
be great [before] God,' or 'he who will struggle with the divine.'[35]

34. Yoreh, "Jacob is named Israel (Twice)."
35. bible.ort.org, "VaYishlach."

4.

A *Remez* Analysis of Israel

4.1. THE SHAPE AND SIZE OF THE LETTERS

In the Torah scrolls, occasionally, some letters are written extra large or small. Excluding those exceptions, not all letters are the same size, with some being larger or smaller. This section examines several examples of letters in the name Israel.

(1) Various Writers

> The twelfth letter of the Hebrew alphabet [ל] is called *lamed*. It has a numeric value of thirty. The pictograph for the *lamed* looks like a lulav branch or a tower soaring in the air. In classical Hebrew script, the *lamed* is constructed [contains the shape] of two letters: a *kaph* (20 = כ) with a *vav* (6 = ו) standing upon it. Therefore, the numerical value of *kaph* + *vav* is twenty-six. That number is the numerical equivalent to the value of the Four-Letter Name of God (the Tetragrammaton): YHVH [10 + 5 + 6 + 5 = 26]. Therefore, concealed within the last letter in Israel is its intimate connection to God.[1]

1. Ginsburgh, *The Wisdom in the Hebrew Alphabet*, 180–91; Munk, *The Wisdom in the Hebrew Alphabet*, 138–42; Raskin, *Letters of Light*, 121–25.

(2) Various Writers

> The letter *lamed* [ל] is unique in the Hebrew alphabet since it is the *tallest* letter. Furthermore, it is the only letter that *rises* above the baseline. Therefore, the *lamed* [ל] hints that people should strive upward to connect with God.[2]

(3) Rabbi Michael L. Munk (1905–1984)

Numerous commentators discuss that the first Hebrew letter in the name Israel is the smallest letter in the Hebrew alphabet and that it symbolizes humility. In contrast, the last letter in the name Israel is the tallest Hebrew letter, the *lamed*. This difference implies that one can ultimately achieve greatness and importance through humility. Greatness and importance are measurable on many levels. For example, Rabbi Munk presents an insight that explains two perspectives on these letters.

> *The Wisdom in the Hebrew Alphabet*
>
> The name ישראל, *Israel*, begins with the smallest letter in the Hebrew alphabet, the י. Conversely, it ends with the tallest letter, the ל. Rabbi Munk concludes that this is to hint or indicate, "that a Jew has the potential to develop from a small child to a great person." He then adds, "the *Aleph-Beis* student can become a great scholar."[3]

(4) Rabbi Aaron L. Raskin (1967-)

> "Yud: The tenth letter of the Hebrew alphabet."
> Furthermore, the *yud* [י, the first letter of the word Israel] looks like a flame that soars ever higher, representing the soul of a Jew yearning to unite with God.[4]

---

2. Ginsburgh, *The Hebrew Letters*, 180–91; Munk, *The Wisdom in the Hebrew Alphabet*, 138–42; Raskin, *Letters of Light*, 122–25.

3. Munk, *The Wisdom in the Hebrew Alphabet*, 141, adapted and modified.

4. Raskin, *Letters of Light*, 101.

(5) Rabbi Moshe Yaakov Wisnefsky

"The Arizal on the Parashah. These letters hint to the elevation and transform from a heel (Ya'akov) to 'a head for me.'"

The first letter of Yisrael [ישראל] is a *yud* [י], the smallest letter in the Hebrew alphabet. The last letter in our name is a *lamed*, the tallest letter in the alphabet. These letters hint to the elevation and transform from a heel (Ya'akov) to "a head for me." [The name Israel can be broken into the word לי ראש [*li rosh spelled lamed yod and resh aleph shin*], "a head for me."]. It must be remembered that, in fact, the origin of the name Yaakov was because he was born holding onto the heel of his twin brother Esav (Bereshit 25:26). Esav identifies this as the way Jacob continues to relate to him—he takes him by the heels.[5]

(6) Rabbi Aaron L. Raskin (1967-)

"Yud: And The Tenth Shall Be Holy."

The *yud* looks like a flame that soars ever higher, representing the soul of a Jew yearning to unite with G-d (*Tanya*, beginning of chapter 19).[6]

(7) Rabbi Aaron L. Raskin (1967-)

"Yud–And The Tenth Shall Be Holy"

Additionally, the *yud* represents the method by which the blessing descends from G-d to His people. The letter *yud* when spelled out is י-ו-ד [*yud vav dalet*]. The *yud* represents a seminal drop, the concentrated power of G-d. The *vav* represents a descent, for its form is that of a chute—and through this the blessings of G-d travel downward to our world. The *dalet*, having height and width, represents the physical world, signifying how G-d's blessings are manifest in every aspect of nature. This teaches us that G-d's blessings don't only reside in heaven. They flow down to this corporeal world and endow us with physical health, sustenance, and success.[7]

---

5. Wisnefsky, "The Arizal on the Parashah."

6. Raskin, *Letters of Light*, 101.

7. Raskin, *Letters of Light*, 101–2.

(8) Various Writers

The size of the first and last letters of Ysrael [ישראל] is instructive and hints at the people's relationship with God. The "tall" [ל] *lamed* hints that God can be transcendent, and the "small" *yod* [י] hints that God can be imminent. These relationships depend upon the people's actions and upholding their end of the covenant.[8]

(9) Various Writers

The size of the first and last letters of Israel [ישראל] are instructive and alludes to the people's possible attitude toward God. The "tall" *lamed* [ל] suggests that people can be arrogant, haughty, and have a puffed-up ego. The "small" *yod* [י] hints that people can be "humble." In contrast, it means to learn and teach! Consequently, the ultimate relationship depends upon the people's thoughts and actions.[9]

4.2. PERMUTATIONS AND ANAGRAMS OF ISRAEL

Prior, Danell identified eight different roots of the first part of the name ישראל . However, the five-letter name of Israel has several significant permutations. The five letters can be combined or rearranged into at least five notable words or phrases.

1. ישראל = Israel = *Ysrael*

2. ראש לי = My head = *Roshi li*

3. ישר אל = Direct to God = *Yashar El*

4. יש ראל = There is 231 = *Yesh Raal*

5. שיר אל = The Secret of God = *Shir El*

---

8. Ginsburgh, *The Hebrew Letters*, 180–91; Haralick, *Inner Meaning of the Hebrew Letters*, 141; Munk, *The Wisdom in the Hebrew Alphabet*, 126, 141; Raskin, *Letters of Light*, 121–25.

9. Blech, *The Secret of Hebrew Words*, 8; Ginsburgh, *The Hebrew Letters*, 180–91; Haralick, *Inner Meaning of the Hebrew Letters*, 141; Munk, *The Wisdom in the Hebrew Alphabet*, 126, 141; Raskin, *Letters of Light*, 121–25.

Kabbalists and the sages take these rearrangements to provide profound insight into these five-letter combinations. Later in this book, an investigation of these combinations follows.

(1) Eleazar ben Judah of Worms—Sefer ha-Hokhmah MS Oxford 1812, fols. 101b–102a (cf. also MS JTS 1786 fol. 43a)

> This is the name of the Shekhinah, as Scripture says: '*Then I was always* [אהיה] *by him, [as one] brought up [by him]*' [Prov. 8:30], which refers to prayer [and] to the sound of prayer, which ascends on high, as Rashi has explained [the verse]: '*And there was a voice from the firmament that [was] over their heads, when they stood [and] had let down their wings*' [Ez. 1:25], which is to be understood as the sound of Israel's prayer, because the prayer ascends to the firmament, which is over their heads; it goes forth and settles on the head of the Holy One, Blessed be He, forming a diadem for Him, as Scripture says: '*He that dwells in the secret place of the most High*' [Ps. 91:1]. 'In the secret place' [בסת"ר] by way of numerology [equals] Akatriel because the prayer sits as a diadem in his place and, [אכתריאל] it is the crown for the head of Akatriel Lord, God of Israel. [...] And the diadem of the Holy One, Blessed be He, [is] 60 myriad thousand parasangs corresponding to the 60 myriad of Israelites, and the name of the diadem is Sari'el, which is an [541 = ישראל] anagram of Israel, which by way of numerology equals 'prayer of one father' [541 = TPeYL"H '"B 'Ch"D] because one patriarch arranges the prayers into a diadem. [...] And Metatron, the Prince of the Countenance, binds crowns [...] as is written in the *Book of the Holy Palaces.*[10]

(2) Rabbi Isaiah Horowitz (1565–1630)

Shney Luchot Habrit

The name יעקב [*Yaakov*] itself actually contains the elements of the mystique of Israel. In the other patriarchs the qualities represented by the name ישראל remained hidden, but during the lifetime of Jacob they were revealed. This was because he was the first of the patriarchs to transmit his heritage to all his children thereby founding a whole and perfect nation. Consider the following about the name ישראל [Yisrael]: All the patriarchs,

---

10. Paluch, "*The Enoch-Metatron Tradition,*" 130.

matriarchs as well as the (12) tribes are alluded to in that name. The first three letters of that name, i.e. ישר , [*yashar*] are the first letters respectively of

1. שרה (Sarah)

2. יצחק (Isaac)

3. רבקה (Rebekah)

They are also the respective first letters of

4. יעקב (Jacob)

5. שבטים (tribes)

6. רחל (Rachel)

The last two in the name ישראל are used only once and represent the first letters in the names

7. אברהם (Abraham) and

8. לאה (Leah)[11]

[Briefly, Israel = ישראל is an acronym for the patriarchs and matriarchs. Therefore, in a sense, the name "Israel" is likened to spiritual DNA (see table 5)].

Table 5. The Anagram of the Name Israel

Hebrew Letters	Transliteration of the Hebrew Letters	Matriarchs and Patriarchs	Hebrew Spelling
י = *yod*	y	Isaac (Yitzhak)	יצחק
		Jacob (Yaakov)	יעקב
שׁ = *sin*	s	Sarah	שרה
ר = *resh*	r	Rachel	רחל
		Rebekah	רבקה
א = *aleph*	'	Abraham	אברהם
ל = *lamed*	l	Leah	לאה

---

11. Horowitz, *Shney Luchot Habrit*, 184. This teaching is found in many places.

(3) Zohar Chadash (c. 1100—c. 1400 CE) and Megaleh Amukos (1637)

> The *Zohar Chadash* (*Shir haShirim*, p. 74) states that there are 600,000 letters in the Sefer Torah which correspond to the 600,000 souls of the twelve tribes of the Jewish people. Similarly, the *Megaleh Amukos* (Va'eschanan #186) writes that the soul of every Jew stems from one of the 600,000 letters in the Torah. The name "Yisrael" itself can be viewed as an acronym for the words, "*Yesh Shishim Ribo Osiyos LaTorah*" ("there are sixty myriads [=600,000] of letters in the Torah").[12]

4.3. *GEMATRIA*: THE NUMERICAL VALUE OF THE FIRST LETTER OF ISRAEL: TEN

The numerical value of *yod* [י], the first letter in Israel, is ten. That number is significant because it is also the first letter in God's name: YHVH. The letter *yod* also represents the Creator, the single point that all of His creation emerges, and the Unity of multiplicity. Moreover, the number ten symbolizes completion, unity, holiness, and sanctity. In the Hebrew Bible and other texts, the number ten is auspicious:

1. With ten sayings or utterances, God created the world.[13]

2. Ten things were created on the first day.

3. Ten generations from Adam to Noah and ten from Noah to Abraham.

4. Ten trials of Abraham.

---

12. Kornfeld, "The Number of Letters in the Torah." One difficulty with these teachings is that there are only 304,804 letters in the Torah. That number is slightly more than half of the number we would expect to find. One way of resolving this contradiction would be to cite another mystical tradition in Ramban's introduction to his *Commentary on the Torah* (for the actual source, see *Yerushalmi Shkalim* 6:1), which refers to a primordial Torah, which preceded the creation of the world. Additional discussion is in Kornfeld.

13. The Ten Sayings are Genesis 1:1, 3, 6, 9, 11, 14, 20, 24, 26, 28, or 2:18. Kaplan, *The Bahir*, 169 writes: There is a question as to what is the tenth saying. Some say that is implied in the first verse, "*In the beginning God created the heaven and the earth*" (*Rosh HaShanah* 32a). This saying parallels Keter-Crown, which is implied but not expressed. Others say that the tenth verse is, "*It is not good for man to be alone*" (Genesis 2:18), and that this corresponds to *Malkhut*-Kingship, which is man's mate (*Bereshit Rabbah* 17:1). This idea is not a dispute, since "the beginning is embedded in the end." Therefore, *Keter*-Crown and *Malkhut*-Kingship are one. This is the head mentioned above (#82 = p. 146).

5. Ten pure animals.

6. The Ten Plagues.

7. The Ten Commandments.

8. The ten spies.

9. The ten days of repentance.

10. The ten *sefirot* (discussed in the Kabbalah).

4.4. *GEMATRIA*: THE NUMERICAL VALUE OF THE FIRST LETTER AND LAST LETTER OF ISRAEL: FORTY

The *lamed* [ל] has a numeric value of thirty (30) though the *yod's* [י] value is ten (10). Together these two letters total forty. In Scripture, the number forty appears numerous times and is auspicious. Conspicuously, it represents a change, a new life, new growth, and transformation. In Scripture, the number forty symbolizes a period of probation testing or trial. Here too, Jacob as a person or the personification of the children of Israel (*B'nei Yisrael*) would result in a lifetime of testing and trial. Jacob's name change represents a transition.

1. The Great Flood lasted forty days and forty nights.

2. Moses fasted forty days in preparation for receiving the Torah.

3. The Israelites wandered the desert for forty years.

4. Manna rained on the Israelites for forty years.

5. The prophet Elijah walked forty days and nights to receive his public ministry.

6. Saul, David, and Solomon each ruled for forty years.

7. Goliath taunted Israel for forty days.

8. There are forty days between the first day of Elul, when we begin to blow the shofar to prepare for Rosh HaShanah, until Yom Kippur, the end of the annual *teshuvah* (repentance) period.

4.5. *GEMATRIA* of the Number Twenty-Six and the Concealment of God's Name

The numerical value of God's four-lettered name YHVH is twenty-six.[14] The number twenty-six is a divine golden thread embedded in the Hebrew Bible, the Siddur (prayer book), and the Jewish liturgy. The writers of these works deliberately interwove God's "presence" in their texts to enrich, spiritually uplift, and imbue them with power. These occurrences are remarkable. The writings contain a latent message hidden in the text through the symbolism of the letters and numbers. A knowledgeable reader familiar with such techniques can unlock these treasures.

1. The *gematria* of YHVH (10 + 5 + 6 + 5) is twenty-six.

2. The letter *Aleph*, representing God's unity, is formed with two *yods* (20) and a *vav* (6), totaling twenty-six.

3. Reinforcing this teaching, the twenty-sixth Hebrew letter in the Torah is an *aleph* in the word *ha'aretz* (the earth).

4. YHVH appears 1820 times in the Torah, equal to 70 x 26.[15]

5. The twenty-sixth verse of the Bible speaks of the image of God. Genesis 1:26 Then God said, "*Let Us make man in Our image, according to Our likeness.*" [NASB][16]

6. Scripture states that God made Eve from Adam's rib. Therefore, metaphorically speaking, He took (subtracted from) Adam (Genesis 2:21—23). If we subtract the value of Eve's name (19) from Adam's (45), we get twenty-six.

7. The creation of woman (Genesis 2:21–22) is detailed in twenty-six Hebrew words.

8. *Teivah* (*Tay-vah*) n. Ark. In Genesis (*Parashat Noah*), chapters 6–9, *teivah* appears twenty-six times.

9. Shem had twenty-six sons, grandsons, and great-grandsons (Gen 10:21–31)

14. Incidentally, twenty-six is also the "English *gematria*" of *God*, since the letter *g* is the 7th of the alphabet, *o* is the 15th, and *d* the 4th, making 26.

15. See Sebag, "Divine Signature—1820." Sebag's computer search identifies numerous examples of 1820. Readers should purchase his text, *Torah Numerology Book*.

16. Lined up vertically, YHVH, forms the stick figure of a human being. *Yod* forms the head, *He* the arms, *Vav* the vertebral column/torso, and *He* the legs.

10. The numerical values of Adam (45), Noah (58), and Abraham (248), the three pillars of Genesis, add up to 351. That number is the sum of the numbers from 1 to 26.

11. There were twenty-six generations from Adam to Moses.

12. The names of the patriarchs and matriarchs contain twenty-six Hebrew letters: Abraham (5), Isaac (4), Jacob (4), Sarah (3), Rebecca (4), Rachel (3,) and Leah (3).

13. Exodus 3:14 = "*God said to Moses,*" *wyamr alhym al mšh* (fifteen letters) "*I AM WHO I Am,*" [NASB] *ahyh ašr ahyh* (eleven letters). These words contain twenty-six letters.

14. The *gematria* values of Abraham's descendants are all multiples of twenty-six in descending order, which ultimately culminates in Joseph:

    1. יצחק | Isaac: 208 (8×26)

    2. יעקב | Jacob: 182 (7×26)[17]

    3. יוסף | Joseph: 156 (6×26)[18]

This descent occurs on three levels: (1) descendants of Abraham: son, grandson, and great-grandson (2) the *gematria* of their names, and (3) the length of time residing in *Eretz Ysrael*.

15. Divine oracle was given to Jacob in Genesis 46:3–4 (twenty-six Hebrew words) *He said, "I am God, the God of your father; do not be afraid to go down into Egypt, for I will make you a great nation there. I will go down with you to Egypt, and I will also surely bring you up again; and Joseph will close your eyes."* [NASB]

16. The first letters of the first three words in the Priestly Benediction (Num 6:24 and in the Siddur) have a *gematria* of twenty-six which is the gematria of God's Four-Letter Name. Verse 1 contains three words and fifteen letters:

"*The LORD bless you, and keep you.*" [NASB] [יברכך יהוה וישמרד]

17. Eleazar Ben Judah of Worms, in his commentary about the *korbon* in his *Siddur Rokeach* says, "In the beginning" (בראשית) until "the sixth day" (יום הששי) the beginning letters of each verse add up to the letters in the name 182] יעקב].

18 Zion is another name for Israel. The number 156 is also the gematria of Zion [*tsade* (90) + *yod* (10) + *vav* (6) + *nun* (50)]. Joseph made his brothers swear to him on his deathbed to take his remains upon their future redemption from Egypt so that he could be buried in Israel (Zion), his homeland. His request reflects how he was a Zionist even though he lived most of his life outside Israel.

17. The *gematria* of the divine designation, *K'lal Ysrael, the "assembly/ congregation of Israel"* [קהל ישראל] totals 676. That number equals 26 x 26.[19]

18. Psalm 136, known as *Hallel HaGadol* [the Great Hallel], contains the refrain *"For His lovingkindness is everlasting"* [NASB] is repeated twenty-six times.

19. Hannah's prayer to God requesting a child contains twenty-six words (1 Sam 1:11).

20. There are twenty-six verses in the Bible that contain all twenty-two letters of the *Aleph-Bet* (Baal HaTurim, Numbers 11:13).[20]

21. The Ten Commandments occupy exactly twenty-six lines. This fact is also why the composers of the Amidah placed 182 (7 x 26) letters in the opening Avot prayer and invoked the Tetragrammaton twenty-six times during the weekday Amidah.

22. The first verse of the *Mah Tovu* prayer contains twenty-six Hebrew letters.[21]

23. There are twenty-six Hebrew letters in the Amidah prayer identifying the patriarchs:

אלהי אברהמ אלהי יצחק ואלהי יעקב

24. In the nontraditional Amidah, there are twenty-six Hebrew letters listing the patriarchs and matriarchs: Abraham (5), Isaac (4), Jacob (4), Sarai (3), Rebecca (4), Rachel (3,) and Leah (3).

25. In the "*Brachah Avot*" of the Amidah are 182 letters = 7x 26.

26. On each *tzitzit* (tassel) are thirty-nine windings (7+8+11+13 separated by double knots). The first three numbers add up to twenty-six. Twenty-six is the numerical value of YHVH.

27. *Shulchan Oruch Orach Chaim* 24 (4, 5) says

> 4 Some have a custom to look at their *Tzitzit* when they reach the verse "And you shall see them," and to place [their *Tzitzit*] on their eyes. This is a beautiful custom. Addition: Some have the

---

19. Lev 16:17; Deut. 31:30; Josh 8:35; 1 Kgs 8:14, 55; 1 Kgs 12:3; 2 Chron 6:3.

20. Exod 16:16; Deut 4:34; Josh 23:13; 2 Kgs 4:39, 6:32, 7:8; Isa 5:25, 66:17; Jer 22:3, 32:29; Ezek 17:9, 38:12; Hosea 10:8, 13:2; Amos 9:13; Zeph 3:8; Zech 6:11; Eccl 4:8, Esth 3:13, Dan 2:45, 3:22, 4:20, 7:19; Ezra 7:28; Neh 3:7; 2 Chron 26:11

21. The prayer is recited by upon entering the synagogue; in the Western Ashkenazi rite.

custom to kiss their *Tzitzit* when they look at them, and all of this is a way of showing love for the Mitzvah (*Beit Yosef*).

5 When one looks upon the *tzitzit* he should look at the two fringes in front of him that have ten knots in total that remind him of his existence, and they also have sixteen strings and ten knots that count as twenty-six as in the [letters in the] divine name.

28. The Mourners Kaddish prayer opens with twenty-six Hebrew words.[22]

29. The first seven words in the Shabbos liturgy, *L'cha Dodi* contains twenty-six Hebrew letters: *L'Cha* (3) / *dodi* (4) / *liKrat* (5) / *kallah* (3) / *p'nei* (3) / *Shabbat* (3) / *n'Kabelah* (5).[23]

(1) Divine Bookend

Noteworthy, the first letter of the Tetragrammaton (YHVH) [and Israel] is the letter *yod* [י]. The letter *yod* is thus employed, representing God's name. The *lamed* [ל], in contrast, the last letter of Israel, is formed out of a *kaph* (כ = number 20) and *vav* (ו = number 6), totaling twenty-six.[24] Thus, within the name of Israel, the divinity of God is concealed. In effect, the first and last letters are divine-like bookends.

(2) The *Bet* and *Lamed* of the Torah

The first letter of the Torah is the letter *Bet* of *Bereshit*. Kabbalist and Sages devote thousands of pages to this letter.[25] They point out that the three lines of a *Bet* form a *Dalet* and *Vav*. Their respective *gematria* is four and six. These two numbers added together equal ten. That number corresponds to the first letter of the Tetragrammaton, God's name. The *lamed* [ל], in contrast, the last letter of Israel, is formed out of a *kaph* (כ = number 20) and *vav* (ו = number 6), totaling twenty-six. Therefore, within these two letters we are taught that YHVH is the first and YHVH is the last.

22. Scherman, *Kaddish*, 26–27.

23. The song is also an acrostic, with the first letter of the first eight stanzas spelling the author's name: Shlomo Halevi Alkabetz, a 16th century kabbalist.

24. Munk, *The Wisdom in the Hebrew Alphabet*, 138; Raskin, *Letters of Light*, 123.

25. Alter, *Why the Torah Begins,"* 192–96.

4.6. *GEMATRIA*: THE NUMERICAL VALUE OF THE FIRST AND LAST LETTER OF THE TORAH: THIRTY-TWO

The Torah begins with the letter *bet* of *Bereshit* and ends with the letter *lamed* [ל] in the word *Israel* [ישראל]. The combination of these two auspicious letters reveals the means God created the world: the letters of the alphabet and the ten *sefirot*. The *gematria* of the combination of these two letters is thirty-two.

1. God's name [*Elohim*] appears thirty-two times in the creation story [Genesis 1:1–2:4].

2. The number thirty-two reveals the means God created the world: the letters of the alphabet and the ten *sefirot*.

3. There are thirty-two pathways between the ten *sefirot* and twenty-two letters of the Hebrew alphabet.

4. There are thirty-two hermeneutic rules of R. Eliezer b. Yose ha-Gelili.

5. The numerical value of the first [*bet* = 2] and last letter [*lamed* = 30] of the Torah total thirty-two.

6. The letter *pe*, meaning mouth, is concealed within the white space of the *bet*.[26] The letter *pe* resembles a mouth, with a tooth emerging from its upper jaw. The adult mouth has thirty-two teeth corresponding to the pathways of wisdom.

7. The number thirty-two relates to human anatomy. The human spine is generally composed of thirty-two vertebrae.

8. The number thirty-two relates to human anatomy. The word heart [*lev*] has a numerical value of thirty-two. This number hints that there are thirty-two words in advance of the first appearance of the word *tov*—good, in the Torah.

9. The number thirty-two is the *gematria* of *kavod* (glory).

10. During the Ring Ceremony, the groom's giving and the bride's acceptance of a ring is the central act of *kiddushin* (holiness). With the ring, the groom accomplishes *kinyan* and "acquires" the bride. The marriage formula is, "By this ring, you are consecrated to me (as my wife) in accordance with the traditions of Moses and Israel." This formula, called the *haray aht*, contains thirty-two letters. As previously mentioned, in

26. Ginsburgh, *The Hebrew Letters*, 255. He also cites *Mishnat Soferim* (in *Mishnah Beruah* 36).

Hebrew, the number thirty-two is written with the letters *lamed* and *bet*, which spell the word that means "heart"—*lev*. Thus, the groom gives his heart as he recites the formula.

(1) Rabbi Eleazar ben Judah of Worms (1160–1238)

Sefer ha-Shem (MS British Museum 737, fol. 203a)

Thus there are thirty-two [three *yods* = 30 + *bet* = 2] to inform us that [God] created the world by the means of thirty-two paths. Therefore, the Torah begins with the *bet* of *Bereshit* and ends with the [*lamed* of] *yisra'el* [*yisra'el*]. Thus, there are thirty-two (*lamed-bet*), which is the numerical value of [the word] *kavod* (glory). There is no glory but the Torah (*'ein kavod 'ela' torah*).[27]

(2) Rabbi Eleazar ben Judah of Worms (1160–1238)

Sefer ha-Hokhmah

And so too, it [the name *Elokim*] is stated thirty-two times in the Act of Creation. So too, there are thirty-two expressions of praise in Psalm 148.[28] So too, there are thirty-two teeth in the mouth. [This is] Because every person should refine himself a good heart for the Torah which corresponds to the thirty-two pathways through which the world was created as it says in Isaiah 26: *Within God is the Rock of creation.*[29]

(3) Rabbi Eleazar ben Judah of Worms (1160–1238)

Perush Sodot ha-Tefillah (MS Paris-BN 772, fol. 163b)

[This prayer *Ha-Yom Harat Olam*] has thirty-two words, corresponding to the thirty-two paths [of wisdom] by means of which the world was created. . . Therefore, the name [YHVH] is written with three *yods*, which equal thirty, and the crown is like a *bet* [which equals two]; thus, there are thirty-two, corresponding to the numerical value of *kavod* . . . May God have mercy on us through the merit of the Torah, which begins with the *bet*

27. Eleazar ben Judah of Worms, *Sefer ha-Shem*, 254.

28. Psalm 148 contains thirty-two praises from such things as the heavens, sun, moon, and angels.

29. Eleazar ben Judah of Worms, *Sefer ha-Hokhmah, Gate 11 Beginnings and Endings.*

of *Bereshit* (Genesis 1:1) and ends with the *lamed* of *le'eine kol yisrae'el* (Deuteronomy 34:12).[30]

(4) Rabbi Asher ben Jehiel (1250–1327)

Sefer Hadar Zekenim

The Torah starts with a *bet* [of *Bereshit*] and ends with a *lamed* [of Israel] [ישראל]: these are [refer to] the thirty-two chambers or channels of the heart. This means to say: Guard the Torah and your heart will be guarded. As it [Prov 3:2] is stated: '*For it is your life and it will lengthen your days.*'[31]

(5) Midrash HaGadol (14th century)

The Torah begins with a *bet* (2 = ב) and finishes with a *lamed* (=ל 30) to tell you that it corresponds to the thirty-two wondrous paths, which correspond to the twenty-two letters [of the Hebrew alphabet] and the ten *sefirot* [that God created the universe].[32]

(6) Gershom G. Scholem (1897–1982)

The Origins of the Kabbalah

For Nachmonides, the ten sefiroth are the "inwardness" of the letters. The beginning and the end of the Torah together form, according to a mystical pun, the "heart," לב, of creation; in terms of gematria, the traditional mysticism of numbers, the numerical value of the word (thirty-two) also indicates the thirty-two paths of wisdom active in it. This "heart" is nothing other than the "will" of God itself, which maintains the creation as long as it acts in it. For it becomes the Nothing, בל, (the inversion of the same two letters), as soon as the will reverses its direction and brings all things back to their original essentiality, "like someone who draws in his breath." But this return of all things to their proprietor is also their return to the mystical pure nothingness.[33]

---

30. Eleazar ben Judah of Worms, *Sefer ha-Shem*, 253.

31. Jehiel, *Sefer Hadar Zekenim*.

32. *Midrash haGadol, Bereshit*.

33. Scholem, *The Origins of the Kabbalah*, 449.

(7) Rabbi Elijah Kitov [Avraham Eliyahu Mokotow] (1912–1976)

Sefer haParahot

The Torah begins with a *bet* and ends with a *lamed* in order to tell you that if you connect them together you will come up with two combinations: בל (*bal*) and לב (*lev*). Meaning to say: בל is the attribute of humility [Because *bal* means "without"]. A person has to appear as nothing in his own eyes. בל is the attribute of truth [because] the mouth and heart [לב] of a person should be equal with his actions. The Holy One, blessed be He says, if a person will fulfill these two attributes [לב and בל], I will look upon him as if he has fulfilled the entire Torah from *bet* until *lamed*.[34]

(8) Rabbi Matitahu Glazerson (1937–)

Letters of Fire

Let us consider, for example, the word לב (*lev*, 'heart'), whose gematria is thirty-two. Just as the heart is the source of life for the body, the thirty-two hermeneutic principles of Rabbi Eliezer are the heart of the Torah and through them, we can receive the life that the Torah gives. The letters *bet* and *lamed* are of the first and last letters of the Torah: *Bereshit* [Genesis] begins with ב, and *Devarim* [Deuteronomy] ends with ל . . .

The *Zohar* tells us that the Jewish people, the Torah, and the Holy One, blessed be He, are one. Through the thirty-two hermeneutic principles, one becomes connected to the Torah, which is made up entirely of names of the Holy One, blessed be He. The fact that the Torah is enclosed, as it were, by the letters of the word לב (*lev*, "heart") suggests to us that Torah study depends upon the heart of man, and also upon the thirty-two (לב) principles of interpretation. Why are these two letters found in reverse order, i.e., the ב at the beginning of the Torah and the ל at the end? This is to teach us that only through reviewing his studies, and "going back" over them, can a person connect his heart to the Torah and come to know it through the thirty-two hermeneutic principles.[35]

---

34. Ki-Tov, *Sefer haParahot, Bereshit.*

35. Glazerson, *Letters of Fire*, 14–15.

4.7 *GEMATRIA*: THE SEVENTY NAMES OF ISRAEL

In biblical study, the number seventy is significant. The number seventy symbolizes completion, unity, holiness, and sanctity. In the Hebrew Bible, the number seventy is auspicious: There is something special about the number seventy. Curiously, we see this number coming up over and over in Tanakh, midrash, and Kabbalah:

1. Seventy nations: The Torah (Genesis 10:32) lists seventy descendants of Noah after the Great Flood, comprising humanity's seventy nations.

2. Seventy languages: Humanity comprises seventy nations, each with its language.

3. Seventy members of Jacob's family come to Egypt: Jacob's family numbered seventy souls when it first descended to Egypt (Genesis 46:27).

4. Seventy elders: Moses received instructions from God to gather seventy elders of the Jewish people to stand with him. (Exodus 24:1; Numbers 11:16).

5. The Sanhedrin (the rabbinical high court) in the Land of Israel would consist of seventy judges (Mishnah Sanhedrin 1:6)

6. Seventy "faces" of the Torah: The midrash (Bamidbar Rabbah 13:15) tells us there are seventy valid ways or perspectives of understanding the Torah.

7. Seventy years of exile: The prophet Jeremiah (Jeremiah 29:10) instructed that God promised that after the destruction of the First Temple, there would be seventy years of Babylonian exile, after which God would remember and redeem His people.

8. Seventy holy days: The midrash calculates that there are seventy Biblical holy days in a solar calendar year (note that by rabbinic decree, the celebration of Pesach, Shavuot, and Sukkot are for an extra day in the diaspora, and Rosh HaShanah extends into a second day everywhere):
   52 Shabbats
   7 days of Pesach
   1 day of Shavuot
   1 day of Rosh HaShanah
   1 day on Yom Kippur
   8 days of Sukkot

9. Seventy divine names: In Scripture, God is referred to by many (seventy) names.

10. Seventy names of Jerusalem: The midrash says the Holy City of Jerusalem, the site of the Holy Temple, is referred to by seventy names in Scripture.

11. Seventy full years of a person's life: King David says, *"As for the days of our life, they contain seventy years, Or if due to strength, eighty years . . ."* (Psalm 90:10; Avot 5:21). (NASB)

12. Seventy represents a multiple of 7 X 10. The number ten denotes fullness.

(1) Midrash Zuta (ca. 10th century)

> 1:1. In parallel to the seventy (kinsfolk) who accompanied Jacob into Egypt and in parallel to the seventy languages (spoken by the seventy nations of the world), seventy names were given (as protection) to the people of Israel; as well as to Jerusalem, the Torah and to the Almighty. (See appendix 5 for the list of seventy names.)[36]

(2) Rabbi Eleazar of Worms (1160–1238)

> *Sodei Razya* [*Secret of Secrets*], p. 1, section 70
>
> Seventy are Israel who were chosen from among seventy, as it says (Leviticus 20:26), . . . *and have set you apart from the peoples, that ye should be Mine.* They [Israel] are called *reshit*, beginning: *In the beginning God created* [Genesis 1:1] and *reshit* is none other than Israel, as it says: *Israel is the Lord's hallowed portion, His first-fruits* [*reshit*] *of the increase* (Jeremiah 2:3). *Bereshit* in *gematria* is [equal to] *yisrael bahar ba-amim*, Israel [He] chose among the nations. And they have seventy names, which are enumerated in *Midrash Song of Songs* (*Song of Songs Zuta*, chapter 1) [see appendix 5]. Thus: *Shema Yisrael, Hear O Israel*, is [written with] an enlarged *ayin* [the last letter of the word, *Shema*], as if to say: *shem ayin yisrael*—seventy names—Israel Likewise, seventy names are to be Blessed be He although the Lord is one. From this [we learn that] Israel, despite the seventy names, [that the people] sing to the heavens [that] *the Lord is one* and only, without equal or parallel, and that Israel was chosen among seventy nations and merited seventy *Sanhedrin* who were free of any fault, as it is written (Song of Songs 4:7): *You are*

36. Granot, *"The Seventy Names of Israel."*

all fair, my love; and there is no blemish in you (*Sanhedrin* 36b); *kulakh* [- You are all] in *gematria* is seventy, and Israel is the eye [*ayin*] of the world, and the Blessed be He will not substitute them with another people, as it is written (Deuteronomy 26:18): *And the Lord declared you this day . . .*[37]

4.8 *GEMATRIA*: THE NUMBER 541

The standard *gematria* of Israel [ישראל] is 541. This number is significant. The sages have identified and written insights about that number throughout the ages.

(1) Abraham Abulafia (1240—ca. 1291)

> *Shàarei Sedeq*, MS Leiden 24.3, Cod. Or. 4762 Warner
> Your name will be called Israel [*yisraèl* = 541] in accord with my name, which numerically is the Active Intellect [*sekhel ha-pòel* = 541], for I and you are one thing [*ani we-atah davar ehad*].[38] Moreover, he who joins the name of twenty-six [i.e., YHWH] with Rebekah and the name of twenty-six with Jacob, and when he joins the four of them equal *yisraèl* [the sum of *rivqah* is 307 and *yàaqov* 182, to which one adds 52, that is 2 x YHWH, and the sum of all four is 541, the numerical value of *yisrael*.] The secret is 'Rebekah loves Jacob' (Gen. 25:28), the matter is the conjunction [*hibbur*] of the soul [*nefesh*], which is the mother, with her true son, whose intellect, by means of the names, is together with the Active Intellect, and they are one thing the intellectual conjunction of the human soul and Active Intellect is cast in the mold of Rebekah and Jacob, the mother associated with the Active Intellect and the son with the human soul.[39]

(2) Abraham Abulafia (1240—ca. 1291)

> *Sefer Hayyei ha-'Olam ha-Ba*

37. Rabbi Eleazar of Worms, *Sodei Razya*, 223. See Lifshitz, 233.

38. *Active Intellect* is a term introduced by Aristotelian philosophy. The Active Intellect serves as an intermediary between the divine and human spheres. It represents the highest aspect of human intellect. The *gematria* [300 + 20 + 30 = 350] + [5 + 80 + 6 + 70 + 30 = 191] equals 541.

39. Wolfson, *Language, Eros, Being,* 581n.91.

The Tree of Life is the pre-existent life of the essence, the life of [everything] above and below, and its secret is the power that judges the world, and the parable is known. Insofar as Whereas her numerical value is the holy letters, it is thus stated, she is the Tree of Life for them that lay hold upon her and happy is every-one who holds her fast," which refers to the numerical value of YSR'L (*yisra'el*—Israel), for no other nation upholds the Torah as we do. And the secret of Israel is the Active Intellect.[40]

Comment: Joanne Boerema, in her Master thesis, adds an important insight that *must* be understood. Moshe Idel shows the numerical equivalents Abulafia uses to prove that the Active Intellect is related to Israel. However, she adds: "The second numerology is that of 541: 'happy;' 'Israel' and 'Active Intellect.' The quotation from Proverbs [3:18] is the link between the two values." Elaborating on this crucial point, she says the following.

The identification of the Torah with the Tree of Life is self-evi-dent within Jewish tradition. During the returning of the Torah in the ark, the whole congregation recite:
She is the Tree of Life to those who hold tight to her . . . "[41]

However, Boerema omits the remainder of the verse that is essential: "*And everyone that upholds it is happy.*" The last word in Proverbs 3:18 is M'ShR (*me'ushar*) = *mem* (40) + *aleph* (1) + *shin* (300) + *resh* (200) = 541. Thus, Israel is happy when it *holds* on to the Torah, which is the Tree of Life.

(3) Abraham Abulafia (1240—ca. 1291)

[Comment: The *gematria* of Israel = 541, *haMitzvot* = 541, and *sekhel ha-po'el* (the Active Intellect) = 541]

Ms. Firenze-Laurenziana II:48, fols. 11b-12a
It is known that the truth of the attainment of reality is the comprehension of the divine name, and by its means he will comprehend the commandments, and they point to the Agent Intellect[95] because the comprehension of the Agent Intellect is similar to a candle,[96] which is a 'river'[97] that goes out of Eden'. . . be careful to the wisdom that emerges from the combination found in the letters [available] to whomever knows how to

---

40. Idel, *Language, Torah, and Hermeneutics*, 36. Idel elaborates on the text: "On the other hand, there is the numerology of 541 = M'VShR (*me'ushar*—happy) = YSR'L (Israel) = SKhL HPV'L (*sekhel ha-po'el*—Active Intellect) and the link between the two is provided by the verse quoted from Proverbs [3:18].

41. Boerema, "*Sefer ha-Ot*," 25–26.

combine them, because this is the goal of the wisdom of the man who understands the divine name[98] . . . because the comprehension of the Agent Intellect, found within the 22 holy letters, comprises all the positive and negative commandments, and it is the candle that illumines to every man and is 'the river that goes out of Eden to water the garden'[99] and it shows that within the 22 letters the comprehension of the name is found, and it is, in its entirety, [emerging] out of the combinations of letters, and you will find truly that out of the combination of letters, the known, the knower and knowledge [are one] . . . and whoever comprehends the Agent Intellect gains the life of the world to come and belongs to the secret of the angels of the living God.

95. haMitzvot = 541= sekhel ha-po'el.

96. For this simile for the mystical union between the human intellect and the Agent Intellect, see Idel, *Studies in Ecstatic Kabbalah*, (SUNY Press, Albany, 1989), 13.

97. In Hebrew the consonant of the candle, *ha-ner* are the same as those of river *nahar*.

98. Or God.

99. Genesis 2:10[42]

Idel adds, "The river emerging from Eden and watering the Garden is, quite plausibly, the intellectual flow that descends from the Agent Intellect, which is separated from matter, and is collected by the human intellect."

(4) Rabbi Isaiah Horowitz (1565–1630)

Shney Luchot Habrit

Throughout Scripture, we find several times the verse: . . . the *Mispar katan* [a system of numerical values in which the digit 0 is ignored ed.= Munk] of the word *aleph-lamed-he-yud*, i.e., 1 + 3 + 5 + 1 = 10. The *Mispar katan* of the word ישראל, also amounts to ten, i.e., 1 + 3 + 2 + 1 + 3 = 10. This is the allusion to the statement of our sages that the Presence of G'd does not come to rest on fewer than ten Jews. We have already shown that the number 10 figures greatly in matters related to tithes. When you combine the respective first letters of the ten emanations . . .

42. Abulafia, Ms. Firenze-Laurenziana II:48, fols. 11b-12a. In Idel, "On Paradise in Jewish Mysticism," 1–38.

the total equals the numerical value of 541 = ישראל.[43] [NB The sum of the digits of Israel (541) is 5 + 4 + 1, which is ten.][44]

(5) Rabbi Shimshon of Ostropoli (ca. 1599–1649)

Shemesh U'Magen

And such you will see in a miracle that the initials of the Ten Plagues mentioned above are a *gematria* of (the word) Israel if you combine them with (the phrase) דצ"כ עד"ש באח"ב מ"ב (plus) *gematria* עמ"ו (His nation or people), Israel His nation (or people) because of the letter heads of all the plagues and the acronyms per all the signs.[45]

Explanation:

The Talmudic sage Rabbi Yehudah developed a mnemonic device to remember the Ten Plagues: *D'TZACH ADASH, B'ACHAV*. Different spellings exist for this mnemonic:

DeTzaCh, ADaSh, BeAChaB

Detzakh, Adash, Be'achav

DeZaCh, AyDaSH, BaCHaV

D'tzach, Adash, B'achav

DTz"Ch, AD"Sh, BACh"B

Dzakh Adash B'ahav

Rabbi Yehudah's mnemonic centers on the first letter of the Hebrew name of each plague divided into three groups. Rabbis propose various explanations for these three divisions. They also offer interpretations of the numerical value of the ten letters that total 501. Altogether, ten letters comprise this mnemonic device.

However, all the plagues, except the tenth, are named in one word. That plague, the tenth plague, "the death of the first-born," requires *two* Hebrew words for identification:

b'chocrot (of the firstborn) = בכורות.

makat (death) = מכת (see table 3).

Though, another alternative exists. Rabbi Shimshon discusses incorporating *eleven* letters to symbolize the Ten Plagues

43. Horowitz, *Shney Luchot Habrit*, 184.

44. This methodology of *gematria* is called the "small" numerical value, or *"Mispar Katan"/ "Mispar Katari."* The numerical value is reduced by adding the numbers in the various digit placements together. Thus, the number 3,280 is also 13. Several examples include Mordecai, Esther, and Haman. Also, note that the number ten (*yod*) represents and is symbolic of God's name [יהוה].

45. Shimshon, *Shemesh U'Magen*, 44.

and dividing the plagues into four groups. In the Ten Plagues, God's concealed His means to redeem Israel. Consequently, the name Israel is interconnected intimately with the Ten Plagues.

Specifically, the nation of Israel is hinted at in the Ten Plagues by adding the numerical value of the first letters of all the plagues *plus* the two letters from the first two words of the tenth plague. Consequently, the numerical value of the initials of the ten plagues increases by forty with the inclusion of the letter *mem* of *makat* (מכת), spelled *mem kaph tav*.[46] Thus, the total is 541, the same value as the word ישראל, Israel.[47] "In other words, using the plagues with which God hit the Egyptians, He healed Israel and extracted them from the impurities of Egypt to be His nation" (see table 6).[48]

In addition, Rabbi Shimshon identifies another miracle. If you add the first letter of each triad plus the *mem bet* of *b'chocrot makat* in a fourth grouping, the total is 116.

דצף עדש באח מב

4 + 70 + 2 + 40 = 116

The same *gematria* of the Hebrew word עמו ("*amo*," spelled *ayin mem vav*) means "His people." *God's ("His") people are the nation of Israel.*[49]

Another source adds that if one employs the *mispar siduri* (ordinal value; e.g., the ordinal value of the letter ש is 21 being the twenty-first letter of the alphabet) of the last letters of each word in Exodus 12:2 [*Parashah Bo*], "*This month shall be unto <u>you</u> the beginning of months; it shall be the first month of the year to <u>you</u>,*" we find:

שהמשׁשׁמןאמיה

21 + 5 + 13 + 21 + 13 + 14 + 1 + 13 + 10 + 5 = 116[50]

The word "you," repeated twice, refers to the people of Israel. Thus, Israel (His people) is concealed twice (based on the numbers 541 and 116) in Rabbi Yehudah's mnemonic device for the Ten Plagues.

Table 6. Rabbi Yehudah's Modified Acronym for the Ten Plagues

46. Boruch, *Ma'amar Sod Etzba Elokim*, 40n9 and 62n26. Additional material based on the teaching of R. Shimshon in his *Shemesh U'Magen*, 1891, page 44; https://www.hebrewbooks.org/7308.

47. The standard methodology of calculating the *gematria* for the Ten Plagues totals 3,280, and the initial letters of the Ten Plagues are 501.

48. Boruch, *Ma'amar Sod Etzba Elokim*, 62n26.

49. The Hebrew word *ayin-mem-vav* appears numerous times in the Tanakh, referring to Israel being God's people: Ps 78:71; 135:12; 2 Chr 7:10; and 35:3.

50. Chanoch ben Yaacov, *Parashat Bo: Normal Gematria*, lines 1–4.

Plague	Transliteration	Translation	Acrostic	*Gematria*
דם	*Dam*	Blood	ד	4
צפרדע	*Tz'fardya*	Frogs	ע	90
כנים	*Kinim*	Lice	כ	20
ערוב	*Arov*	Beasts	ע	70
דבר	*Dever*	Cattle Pestilence	ד	4
שחין	*Sh'chin*	Boils	ש	300
ברד	*Barad*	Hail	ב	2
ארבה	*Arbeh*	Locusts	א	1
חשך	*Chosheh*	Darkness	ח	8
בכורות	*B'choro*	Firstborn	ב	2
מכת	*Makat*	Death of the	מ	40
Total				541

(6) Rabbi Ya'avetz of Emden (1697–1776)

The Siddur of Ya'avetz

And the name Israel (ישראל) in *gematria* [541] is equivalent to the twenty occurrences of the Ineffable Name [YHVH] and [plus] the [name of God] "*I shall be*," אהי"ה [*Ehiyeh* is twenty-one]. It appears to me the reason for the *remez* (implication/hint) in the twenty uses of the Ineffable Name corresponds to the letter *Yod* when spelled out [its *miliu*] as יו"ד [*yod, vav,* and *dalet*] which adds up to twenty.[51] This corresponds to the covenant that the Holy One Blessed Be He enacted with Abraham, our Father, of Blessed Memory, corresponding to his ten fingers and ten toes as taught in *Sefer HaYetzirah*. And, therefore, the letter *Yod* is itself doubled (and the number twenty corresponds to a crown (כתר) [*Keter*]. And the Ten Commandments contain letters that add up to twenty). And *gematria* indicates finality for in the art of mystery/secret (*sod*) their ending is really their beginning.

And the Name of God, אהי"ה, [*Ehiyeh*] is included within the above *gematria* to teach us about the Sublime Authority, root of all roots [the name *Havayah*], the beginning and source of all beings. And the name, "*I shall be*" [*Ehiyeh*] adds up to twenty-one in this fashion. But this is certainly (play on words with the

---

51. For example, *yod* is spelled *yod, vav,* and *dalet. Yod* is numerically equivalent to 10, *vav* to 6, and *dalet* to 4.

word אף [*aph*, spelled *aleph pe*] which also adds up to twenty-one) worthy of Israel to teach all about this *gematria* (The word אהיה in a form of *gematria* called א"ת ב"ש—a reverse usage where an *aleph* numerically equals a *tav*—adds up to the letters in the word 620—כתר). [Additionally, the numerical equivalent of *Ehiyeh*, also spells out the word אק, [*aph*, spelled *aleph pe*] meaning "only," referring to the verse (Psalm 73:1): "*God works only good for Israel.*"][52]

(7) Azulai, Chaim David Yosef (1724–1808)

The Mishnah: Avot 1:1 "All Israel have a share in the World to Come"

> The numerical value of the last letters of the words:
> "*Kol Yisrael yeish lahem cheilek le'Olam Haba*" —
> "All Israel have a share in the World to Come"
> (כל ישראל יש להם חלק לעולם הבא)
> is five hundred and forty-one (541), which is also the numerical value of the word "*Yisrael*" (ישראל) to hint that the name "Yisrael shields and saves one to merit *Olam Haba* (World to Come).[53]

(8) Rabbi Yitzchak Ginsburgh (1944–)

> "*Va'eira*: The Angel Micha'el All about Sarah"
> The name "Israel" stems from the root meaning "to overcome" or "to minister" as does the name "Sarah." The numerical value of "Israel" (ישראל) is 541, which is also the sum of "Sarah" [שרה = 505] spelled *Sin resh he*] and "Leah" [לאה = 36] spelled *Lamed aleph he*, the mother of Jacob's six children: ישראל = לאה שרה.[54]
>
> *Kiddushin* 30b
> Our Sages taught: There are three partners in the forming of a person: The Holy One, Blessed be He, who provides the soul, and his father and his mother.
>
> Niddah 31a
> Our Rabbis taught: There are three partners in man, the Holy One, blessed be He, his father and his mother. His father supplies

---

52. *Aph*, spelled *aleph pe* meaning "only," referring to the verse (Psalm 73:1): "God works only good for Israel.

53. Azulai, "All Israel Has a Share in the World to Come."

54. Ginsburgh, "*Va'eira*," lines 20–22.

the semen of the white substance out of which are formed the child's bones, sinews, nails, the brain in his head and the white in his eye; his mother supplies the semen of the red substance out of which is formed his skin, flesh, hair, blood and the black of his eye; and the Holy One, blessed be He, gives him the spirit and the breath, beauty of features, eyesight, the power of hearing and the ability to speak and to walk, understanding and discernment. When his time to depart from the world approaches the Holy One, blessed be He, takes away his share and leaves the shares of his father and his mother with them.[55]

(9) Rabbi Mattityahu Glazerson (1937 –)

Building Blocks of the Soul: Studies of the Hebrew Letters and Words of the Hebrew Language

The nation of Israel is essentially connected to God. If the numerical values of the two names of God—אהיה [*Ehyeh*] (1 + 5 + 10 + 5 + 2 = 21) and יהוה [YHVH] (10 + 5 + 6 + 5)—Are multiplied together (21 X 26 = 546), the total equals the numerical value of ישראל (Israel = 10 + 300 + 200 + 1 + 30 = 541) plus the number (5) of the word's letters (541 + 5 = 546).[56]

(10) Rabbi Yitzchak Ginsburgh (1944-)

"*Va'eira*: The Angel Micha'el—All about Sarah."

It is interesting to note that the name "Isra'el" [ישראל] follows the common naming of an angel (that ends with "*el*"). Indeed, Jacob received the name Israel only after having defeated Esau's angel, "Because you have wrestled with angels and men and you have overcome." Jacob's ability to overcome Esau's angel came by his including the strength of Gavri'el, who manifest the power of the *sefirah* of might. After the sun rose, Jacob was healed by the power manifest in the angel Repha'el.[57]

---

55. *Niddah*, 105.

56. Glazerson, *Building Blocks of the Soul,* 347. Note: When informing Moses about the redemption of Israel, God used these two names (Exodus 3: 14–15).

57. Ginsburgh, "*Va'eira*," lines 14–18.

(11) Rabbi Yitzchak Ginsburgh (1944–)

Living in Divine Space (2003)

The word *et* is composed of two letters, *aleph* and *tav*, the first and the last letters of the Hebrew alphabet, respectively. Both the beginning and the end of Divine service is fear, as it is written: "*The beginning of wisdom is the fear of God*" and "The final word, all having been understood, fear God and observe His commandments, for this is all [i.e., the ultimate life purpose] of man."

The letter *alef*, the first letter of the alphabet, refers in particular to wisdom, *chochmah*, as explicitly stated in the verse, "I will teach you [*a'alefcha*, from the root *alef*] wisdom." This is also indicated by the fact that creation begins with *et*: "In the beginning God created *et* [the heavens …]." In the *Targum Yerushalmi*, "In the beginning" is translated as "With wisdom."

The letter *tav*, the last letter of the alphabet, refers in particular to understanding, *binah*, which, in Kabbalah, is referred to as the World to Come or "the end of days." In *Sefer Yetzirah*, [1:5] *chochmah* and *binah* are known as the "absolute [literally, 'depth of'] beginning" and the "absolute end," respectively. When the numerical values of *chochmah*, 73, and *binah*, 67, are added to that of *et*, 401, the result is 541, the numerical value of *Israel*. Israel is also regarded as the beginning and end of creation, for God created this world for the sake of Israel, in order that Israel inherit the World to Come: "The end of action is the beginning of thought." [*Lech Dodi*][58]

(12) Rabbi Nilton Bonder (1957–)

Boundaries of Intelligence

This text [Genesis 32] not only provides us with the etymology of the word-code Israel but also gives us the context in which is arose. 'Israel' is a word that transcends the designation of a single people to become a sign that someone belongs to an order of spiritually initiated people. In other words whoever belongs to this category can be considered as *'Those who wrestle with God and with men.'*

One Biblical commentary (*Shem Sh'muel*) uses a curious method to make a revealing observation . . .'*gematria*' . . .

The commentary referred to above analyzes the numerical value of the words Jacob and Israel. Two words that represent

---

58. Ginsburgh, *Living in Divine Space*, 59.

not just a change in a name but in Jacob's very essence. What happened numerically between Jacob and Israel? The sum of the letters in Jacob works out to 182 while the numerical value of Israel is 541. The difference between Israel and Jacob is an increase of 359—precisely the numerical value of the word 'Satan' (which means *hindrance* or *roadblock* or, in the mythical sense, *the demon*).

The main idea behind the notion of spiritual intelligence is not that feelings or impulses should be cast out but—to the contrary— that they should be incorporated. When Jacob wrestles with his demons and makes them part of an inner struggle, without needing to demonize his brother, anyone else, or any given situation; when he assumes full responsibility for the reality around him, blaming no one; and when he places his senses and reverences in front of his fears and insecurities, then his name is Israel.[59]

(13) Rabbi Yehoshua Alt (1985–)

"The Fight For The 100 *Brachos*"
We see the idea of 100 *Brachos* from an earlier origin. In the episode of Yaakov fighting with the *Malach*, the Satan (*Malach*) took the 100 Brachos. [The Satan, *Yetzer Hara* and *Malach Hamaves* are one and the same (*Baba Basra* 16a). This is the Malach Yaakov fought with.] The Satan struck the socket of his hip. [Breishis 32:26] כף [The word *qoph*] has a sum of 100. Yaakov's name was therefore changed to [32:29] ישראל since Yaakov symbolizes אמת [*emet* = truth] as it says [Micah 7:20] Adding 100 (*Brachos*) to (אמת) (*emet*) 441 we get a result of 541, the same as ישראל.[60]

(14) Anonymous

The numerical value of Israel (ישראל) is 541 [10 + 300 + 200 + 1 +30]. The number 541 is the product of his father Isaac (= יצחק Yitzchak = *Yod tsade khet qoph* = 208) + his mother Rebekah (307 = רבקה = *Resh bet qoph he*) + YHVH (26 = יהוה).

59. Bonder, *Boundaries of Intelligence*, 58–60.
60. Alt, "The Fight For The 100 Brachos," 2.

(15) Various Sources

The *gematria* of the Hebrew word המצות = "*haMitzvot*," i.e., "The Commandments" is 541. [Numbers 36:13]. So too, is the *gematria* of Israel [ישראל].

(16) Various Sources

The *gematria* of Israel [ישראל] totals 541. Significantly, that number is the 100th prime number. The number 100 is auspicious, being 10^2, the squaring of the first letter *Yod* [י] of God's name (יהוה) [YHVH] (see table 7).

Table 7. The First 100 Prime Numbers

	1	2	3	4	5	6	7	8	9	10
1–10	2	3	5	7	11	13	17	19	23	29
11–20	31	37	41	43	47	53	59	61	67	71
21–30	73	79	83	89	97	101	103	107	109	113
31–40	127	131	137	139	149	151	157	163	167	173
41–50	179	181	191	193	197	199	211	223	227	229
51–60	233	239	241	251	257	263	269	271	277	281
61–70	283	293	307	311	313	317	331	341	347	349
71–80	353	359	367	373	379	383	389	397	401	409
81–90	419	421	431	433	439	443	449	457	461	463
91–100	467	479	487	491	499	503	509	521	523	541

(17) yeshshem.com

"Unity that Comes from Hearing—*Kevanah* for the Word Israel" 541 is also 100 + 441. These numbers correspond to the words *Yamayim* [100 = 10 + 40 + 10 + 40 = ימים] meaning Seas and *Emet* [400 + 40 + 1 = אמת], meaning truth. Seas is a code word in Kabbalah for Torah. Therefore Israel [ישראל] stands for the "Truth of the Torah."[61]

61. Yeshshem.com., "Unity that Comes from Hearing," lines 17–19.

(18) A Combination of Various Sources

In *Bereshit* (Gen.) 28:16 Ya'akov declares, *"There is YHVH in this place!"* Why does he say those precise words? The answer is multifaceted. First, the *gematria* of the phrase *"There is YHVH in this place"* is 541. (See table 8) Thus, this is "the Place" in which YHVH is to be found. Second, the children of Israel can discover and connect to YHVH via His *mitzvot*. The *gematria* of the Hebrew word *"haMitzvot"* is 541. Third, the land promised to Abram (Abraham), and his descendants is *Eretz Yisrael*. The numerical value of Israel is 541. Fourth, YHVH, the name of the LORD, is concealed in the *gematria* of the Hebrew word מקום (*makom*), meaning "place." This result is calculated by squaring the number in which the letters of the word or name are calculated according to their numerical value squared. The Tetragrammaton, YHVH equals = $10^2 + 5^2 + 6^2 + 5^2 = 186$.[62] In turn, the word מקום ("Place") is another name for LORD. Tying this all together, the 186th word in the Torah is אלהים (the name Elohim, translated as God): when *God* made two great lights (Genesis 1:16). Thus, in the place named *Eretz Yisrael*, specifically given by YHVH to the children of Israel, is the place that they can find and connect to God/LORD via His *mitzvot*.

Table 8. *LORD is in this Place*: Genesis 28:16

English	Hebrew	*Gematria*
[The] LORD	יהוה YHVH	10+5+6+5 = 26
is	יש *yes*	10+300 = 310
in this	הזה *Haz-zeh*	5 + 7 + 5 = 17
place	במקום *Ba-makom*	2 + 40 + 100 + 6 + 40 =188
		26 + 310 + 17 + 188 = 541

62. This topic is in *Sefrei ha-Iyyun*, an anonymous text written around the year 1200 in the province of Castile.

5.

A *Derash* Analysis of Israel

(1) Genesis Rabbah (Bereshit) (ca. 500 CE)

Bereshit 1:4

Six things preceded the creation of the world. Some were actually created, and others came up only in God's thought as what was to be created. Torah and the throne of glory were created. The creation of the fathers, Israel, the Temple, and the name of the Messiah came up only in God's thought. R. Ahavah son of R. Ze'ra said: So, too, repentance. And some say: Also, the Garden of Eden and Gehenna.

It is said in the name of R. Samuel son of R. Isaac that the thought of creating Israel preceded all else. Had not the Holy One foreseen that after twenty-six generations Israel would accept the Torah, He would not have written in the Torah: "*Command the Children of Israel*" (Numbers 5:2) or "*speak to the Children of Israel*" (Exodus 25:2).[1]

(2) Jerusalem Talmud, Ta'anit 2:6 (ca. 375–ca. 425 CE)

HALAKHAH: Rebbe Simeon ben Laqish in the name of Rebbi Yannai: The Holy one, praise to him, associated his great name with Israel. {a parable} of a king who had the small key of a

---

1. Freedman, *Midrash Rabbah: Genesis*, 6.

jewelry [to open the door of his palace].[2] The king said, if I leave it as it is, it is apt to be lost. Therefore, I shall put in on a chain. Then if it were lost the key would prove where it is. So the Holy One, praise to Him, said, if I leave Israel as they are, they would be absorbed by the nations. Therefore, I shall associate My great Name with them and they will survive.[3]

(3) Leviticus Rabbah 36:4; Yakut, Isa §452 (5–7th centuries)

The verse, *"But now thus saith the Lord: Jacob created thee, Israel formed thee"* (Isaiah 43:1) [JV: *"But now thus saith the Lord, that created thee, O Jacob, and He that formed thee, O Israel."*] means, so said R. Phinehas in the name of R. Reuben, that the Holy One said to His world: My world, My world, who created you? Who formed you? Jacob created you. Israel formed you.

R. Berekhiah [hastened to explain]: Heaven and earth were created only for the sake of Israel, for it is said, *"On account of the beginning God created"* (Genesis 1:1). Here, by *"the beginning"* is meant Israel, of which Scripture says, *"Israel is the Lord's hallowed portion, the beginning of His harvest"* (Jeremiah 2:3).[4]

(4) Alphabet of Rabbi Akiva (ca. 700–900 CE but ascribed to the Mishnaic-era of Rabbi Akiva)

The Torah commences with the *bet* and ends with a *lamed*, its last words being, *"in the sight of all Israel."* These two letters combined form the word *bal* (nought); reversed, they read *lev* (heart). Thus said God to Israel: If you serve Me in this twofold manner, with a sense of your own nothingness and with your heart (with humility and devotion), I will account it to you as if you fulfilled the entire Torah from the *bet* to the *lamed*.[5]

2. The name Israel includes *El* ("God"), and the name Yehudah includes YHVH ("LORD").

3. Guggenheimer, *The Jerusalem Talmud,* 2:6.

4. Bialik and Ravnitzky, *The Book of Legends,* 334:14.

5. Kasher, *Encyclopedia of Biblical Interpretation,* 1:8

(5) Tanna D'Vei Eliyahu (10th century)

Seder Eliyahu Rabbah, chapter (27) 25
Reading the words of Genesis 32:29, *"Your name shall be called no more Jacob, but Israel,"* the Tanna Devei Eliyahu = taught that one should read "Israel" as *ish ra'ah El*, "a man who sees God," for all of Jacob's actions were directed to God.[6]

(6) Rabbi Abraham Ibn Ezra (ca. 1089–1167?)

Commentary on the Pentateuch—Genesis (Bereshit)
Another Midrash says that the Torah opens with *In the beginning* [בראשית] and closes with the word *Israel* [ישראל] because Israel [ישראל] was on God's mind at the time of creation.[7]

(7) Rabbi Eleazar ben Judah of Worms (1160–1238)

Sefer ha-Hokhmah
Bereshit [begins with a *bet*] and the end of the Torah [is the *lamed* in] *Yisrael* (Israel = ישראל). And so too [the first letter of the second word of the Torah starts with a *bet*, *BR'*, pronounced *Bara*] and [the last letter of the second to the last word in the Torah is the *lamed* in the word *Khl* [pronounced *kal*]. And, once again [you have] *lamed bet lamed bet*. For each person has two hearts, as it is stated in Deuteronomy 6:5, *"You shall love the Lord your God with all your heart"* [The word "hearts" is plural.].[8]

(8) Rabbi David ben Abraham (1212–1300)

Midrash David Hanagid
And further our sages say: That He, blessed be He; He started the Torah with a *bet* and finished it with a *lamed* because the letters together spell the word *lev* [which means heart]. This is to teach you that a person cannot learn Torah and comprehend

6. Braude, *Tanna Debe Eliyyahu*, 302.

7. Abraham ibn Ezra, *Ibn Ezra's Commentary on the Pentateuch*, Introduction, 17. See Midrash Rabbah 1:4

8. Rabbi Eleazar ben Judah of Worms, *Sefer ha-Hokhmah*, Gate 11: Beginnings and Endings and Endings and Beginnings/*Rosh ve-Sof* and *Sof ve Rosh*).

its secrets and understand it [the Torah] if his heart [*kavanah*, intention] is incomplete.[9]

(9) Rabbi Avraham Saba (1440–1508)

Tzror Hamor Torah Commentary
The name "Yaakov" is associated with the Jewish people's exile experiences, whereas the name "Israel" [ישראל] is linked with the periods when the Jewish people live in their own land and are masters thereof.[10]

(10) Rabbi Ephraim ben Aaron Luntshits (1550–1619)

Kli Yakar
"And he said, 'Your name will no longer be Yaakov, but rather Yisrael [ישראל].'"—This expression means *"yashar E-l"* (God is upright), for *"yashar"* indicates seeing, as in the verse "I see him (*ashurenu*) but not from close." He is thereby telling him that Yaakov sees God's face, and the angel has not succeeded in blinding him to the reality of God. In declaring that he has *"striven with God,"* he uproots the name Yaakov from him, for "Yaakov" hints to *"The heart is deceitful (akuv) above all, and weak"* (*Yirmiyahu* 17:9), whereas "Yisrael" expresses the idea of *"mishor"* (a straight place), as it is said of the future (*Yirmiyahu* 40:4), *"The crooked shall be made straight."* And not something that appears straight [only] in human eyes, but something that appears straight in the eyes of both God and man. Therefore, he says, *"You have striven with God and with men"*—for it is by virtue of your actions that you will be a prince and ruler with God and with men and you shall prevail. This is the meaning of "Yisrael"—*yashar E-l*; a *mishor* that appears straight in the eyes of God, as well.[11]

(11) Rabbi Yaakov Culi (1689–1732)

MeAm Lo'ez (Genesis 32, 29)

9. David ben Abraham Maimuni, *Midrash David Hanagid*.

10. Saba, *Tzror Hamor*, 2:603.

11. Ephraim Solomon ben Aaron Luntshits, *Kli Yakar*, lines 43–54.

"God said: Your name shall no longer be Jacob, but Israel for you have fought with beings both divine and human and have prevailed."

This is what the angel told Jacob: The Holy One Blessed Be He is about to reveal Himself to you at Beth El to inform you that your name shall no longer be *Ya'akov*, but rather Israel, as we will see later in chapter 5. And the reason is that [you] are acquainted with the Godly angels, and you are important in the presence of the Holy One, and you struggled/wrestled with strong men, namely Lavan and Esau, people who [seemingly] have advantage and ability. And your face is engraved into the seat of glory on high, and you *struggled* and fought with the military general of Esau, who is an angel, and you attained victory over him.[12] And until now your name was *Ya'akov* (יעקב in Hebrew), a name associated with deceit and trickery (*akav*), and it is possible to think that you attained the blessings [of the birthright] through trickery and deceit. But from now moving forward, your name shall be Israel, that can be interpreted as ישר אל—uprightness to God—as the Holy Be Blessed Be He Himself is standing at the ready to bless you in Beth El (literally: the House of the Lord), and then I, too will agree to your blessings. Furthermore, since a change of name heralds and brings much benefit and value towards eradicating the decree, as we have seen in *Parashat Va-Yera*, and therefore if the decree had been that you would be killed at the hands of Esau, now that your name is Israel, you shall rest assured and should not fear.[13]

(12) Rabbi Moshe Hayyim Ephraim of Sudilkov (1740–1800?)

Degel Mahane

It is written in the Zohar, "God, Torah, and the souls of Israel are all one" (Zohar 2.73b). This needs to be understood. The very life of Israel (*hiyut Yisrael*) is, as it were, is from the essence of God (*m'azmut Kudshe B'rikh Hu*),[25] as it is written, *and He blew into his mouth the soul of life (nishmat hayyim)* (Genesis 2:7).[26] And we know that a person only breathes from his essence. *And this is the Torah* (Numbers 19:14) this is Adam/

---

12. The Hebrew word for "great" here is *sar-itha* (שרית) [spelled *sin resh yod tav*]. It can also mean to "struggle" or to "contend." "God" here is *Elohim* which also denotes angels and judges.

13. Culi, *Me'am Loez*, Genesis 32, 29. Note: Changing one's name can also help to annul a decree.

man. Therefore (the Torah) has 248 positive commandments and 365 negative commandments that correspond to the limbs and sinews of the human body. This is how to read the verse *And this is the Torah, Adam* (Numbers 19:14).[27] This alludes to the fact that the Torah is literally (*mamash!*) the essence of Adam/Israel—God the Torah and Israel are one.[28]

[25] See, *Degel Mahane Ephraim* (Jerusalem, 1994), 32b where he teaches that the life-force of God is present in the natural world. I would suggest, however, that the dimension of divine life in Israel, noted here as "essence," is of a different nature than the divine life-force in natural world.

[26]Cf. Shneur Zalman of Liadi, *Sefer HaTanya*, chapter 2, p. 6.

[27]A more common translation of this verse would be, *This is the teaching about a person [who dies in a tent]*. See Robert Alter, *The Five Books of Moses: Translation and Commentary* (2004). The *JPS Tanakh* translates it more colloquially. *This is the ritual when a person dies in a tent.*

[28]*Degel* (Jerusalem, 1994), p. 1. On rabbinic notions of the Torah as God incarnate, see Jacob Neusner, *The Incarnation of God* (1992), especially pp. 82–100; 150–98. On Logos Theology, and Boyarin, *Border Lines*, pp. 112–27. Cf, Wolfson, "Judaism and Incarnation: The Imaginal Body of God," *Christianity in Jewish Terms*, pp. 239–53.[14]

(13) Moses [Moshe] Sofer (Schreiber) (c. 1785–1835)

Chatam Sofer on Torah

Vayishlach 20: *Your name shall no longer be Jacob, but Israel,* The names *Yaakov* and *Yisra'el* in *gematria* (a system in which each letter is represented numerically) correspond to the words *Kar'a Satan* [קרע עטן]. (Translator's addition: *Kar'a Satan* means "may Satan be torn asunder" and this is also the acronym for the verses recited during at the Shofar ceremony as we sound the first blasts of the shofar on Rosh HaShanah). This is a name that is capable of eradicating the externals and therefore the minister of Esau said that name is the source of the externals. Your name shall no longer be called Ya'akov, but Yisrael, namely solely and exclusively Yisrael, so that it would not be possible to eradicate the externals, but the Blessed Name said that "your name is Jacob, etc." so that the power to eradicate and cancel would still be extant.

14. Moshe Hayyim Ephraim of Sudilkov, *Degel Mahane*, 9.

Vayishlach 21: *You must not ask my name,* in my humble opinion it is well known that which the author of the *Pela'ah* [Rabbi Pinchas Horowitz] said regarding Mano'ach, where the Angel of God told him: "you must not ask for my name; it is unknowable (here the word *Peli* is translated, but according to many interpretations this is the precise name of the angel)," that the names of Angels change based on their specific mission. Based on the purpose and type of mission, their respective name is chosen. And regarding Mano'ach, the specific mission of the Angel was to cause a vow of the Nazirite oath to be placed upon his son Samson who was just born to him, therefore the Angel said that "you must not ask my name," for it changes each time and it is wonder and an amazement that now his name is "Peleh" in recognition of the fact that he will bring about an oath to be affirmed. Based on this, we can comment that it is well-known that we often find the letter *yod* [appended to certain words] such as we find in Psalms 114:8—*"who turned the rock"* (where the first word ההפכי has an *yod* added)—as well as many other cases, for the honor and glory of the language. Here in our case [in *Vayishlach*] the crux of the mission of the Angel was to bestow the name of *Yisra'el* upon him and to thank him for the blessings which Isaac had bestowed as can be seen in Rashi. And the main purpose of his duty was "for the name" [In Hebrew this is [לשם, namely the bestowal of the name Yisrael which was now being given to Ya'akov, and therefore the Angel said: *"you must not ask my name"* (Hebrew: name—לשמי], now [for this purpose and this mission] my name is now לשם. This can be interpreted as meaning "for the purpose of [giving] the name" and this his name now "in my name" [לשמי] and the *yod* is added.[15]

(14) Rabbi Judah Aryeh Alter [of Ger] (1849–1905)

Sefat Emet

In the verse (Genesis 32:25), *"And a man wrestled with him until the break of dawn,"* our Sages of Blessed Memory interpreted this verse that their feet raised the dust and dirt from the ground until the seat of glory and honor. This is a hint that the war between Satan and the Evil Inclination is always in line

---

15. Sofer, *Chatan Sofer on Torah—Bereshit*, (*Vayishlach* 20 and 21). Note: Esau's angel changed Yaakov's name to Yisrael, being a composite of two words, אל (God) and שיר (song). Specifically, the final letters of Yisrael, אל are derived from the angel's name and the letters "שיר" are based on the angel's mission to sing praises to Hashem.

with what our Sages said that someone who is bigger [in terms of morals and values] from his friend, this person's inclination is also higher and more exalted and therefore righteous people are compared to a mountain. The power of battle and fighting always reaches until the seat of glory and honor. And therefore, our Sages said that repentance (*teshuvah*) is on a higher level as it is able to penetrate and touch the seat of glory and honor, for the flaw [in one's actions] progresses to there as well. And there in the root of the soul of Man is Ya'akov whose visage is engraved and inscribed under the seat of glory and honor, a place where flaw is not present, and from there *teshuvah* emanates. And therefore, after this war/battle, the angel told Ya'akov that "your name shall no longer be Ya'akov," for Ya'akov is his *Nom de Guerre* and since he emerged from this battle victorious, he merited to be called by the appellation, Israel.[16]

(15) Rabbi Judah Yudel Rosenberg (1859–1935)

Sefer Peri Yehuda

BR'SYT: To connect the end of the Torah with its beginning through words and letters. The two words are *Israel* and *Bereshit*, and the two letters are *lamed* and *bet*, and everything is one. It is stated in the holy *Zohar* (Pinchas 220a) that Israel [ישראל] amongst the nations of the world is compared to a heart inside the body: "The Holy One Blessed be He made Israel a heart for the whole world and thus Israel amongst the other nations is like a heart amongst other bodily organs. Just like the other parts of the body are unable to exist at all even one minute without the heart, so too, all the nations are not able to exist at all without Israel." It is known and understood that the reason that the existence of the other nations and the life that Israel gives to the other nations is because they receive the Torah which is the source of life of the entire world. For this is the condition the Holy One, blessed be He made when He created the world—that if Israel will receive the Torah, the world will be sustained.[17]

(16) Rabbi Baruch ha-Levi Epstein (1860–1941)

Torah Temimah

16. Alter [of Ger], *Sefat Emet*, Genesis, *Vayishlach* 32.

17. Rosenberg, *Sefer Peri Yehuda*. See. Bereshit.

32:29 *with God* [*Elokim*] etc.– Rabba said a hint hinted to him, that two ministers (or regents) were destined to come out of him—the head of the Exile [*galut*] in Babylonia [alluded to by "*Elokim*"] and the *Nasi* [president] in *Eretz Yisrael* [alluded to by "*anashim*"]. The exile was thus hinted to him (Hullin 92a).[18]

(17) Rabbi Julian Morgenstern (1881–1977)

A Jewish Interpretation of the Book of Genesis
But with the morning dawn came victory, victory and blessing. *"Thy name shall be called no more Jacob, but Israel; for thou hast striven with God and with men, and hast prevailed."* With this earthly nature, to the voice of men so often hearken, Jacob had striven during these twenty years, and particularly during this last night, and it had not prevailed; he had conquered it. With the divine voice within, the voice of God, Jacob had striven, too, and at last, after a bitter struggle, it had prevailed. He had entered upon the struggle twenty years before, a selfish, deceitful young man. Now he emerged from it, purified, noble, victorious, but also old, wearied and limping; yet erect and happy withal. He was a different, a new, a better man; and as a symbol thereof came the new name; no longer Jacob, "the Deceiver," but Israel, "the Champion of God," who was henceforth to fight the battles of the Lord, and become a blessing unto all mankind.[19]

(18) Anonymous Hasidic work (1928)

Kitvei Qodesh
'*Then* [*God*] *said to him:* "*Your name shall no longer be called Jacob, but Israel (YiSRaèL)*"' (Genesis 32:29), i.e., *LY Ro'Sh* ('I have a head'), [meaning] that one should always be conscious (*besechel*) [of what one is doing]. '*He said: "Let me go, for the dawn is breaking"*' (Genesis 32:27)—that is to say if a person has awe of the Creator—blessed be [God]—one has no desire for anything physical, but is [on the contrary] separated from the physical. Hence, "*Let me go, for the dawn is breaking*"'—the meaning [is that this is] an

18. Epstein, *Torah Temimah*, Genesis 32.29.
19. Morgenstern, *A Jewish Interpretation of the Book of Genesis*, 271–72.

expression of being divested, for one is divested of the physical for 'the dawn is breaking' and 'the dawn' [represents] awe.[20]

(19) Rabbi Aryeh Kaplan (1934–1983)

Sefer Yetzirah The Book of Creation: In Theory and Practice

[Background information] Tradition declares that the Torah is the blueprint of creation. As pointed out numerous times, the first letter of the Torah is the *Bet* [ב] of *Bereshit* [בראשית]— commonly translated as *"In the beginning."* In contrast, the last letter of the Torah is the *Lamed* [ל] of *Yisrael* (ישראל)—*"Israel."* Together, these two letters also spell the Hebrew word *lev* (לב) [spelled *lamed bet*], meaning heart. When reversed, they spell the word *bal*, meaning nothingness.

Rabbi Aryeh Kaplan, in his commentary on *Sefer Yetzirah*, discusses another unique distinction these two letters, the *Lamed* (ל) and *Bet* (ב), also share. Both letters can serve as a prefix: *lamed* means "to," and *bet* means "in." Kaplan elaborates that the three letters of the Tetragrammaton, the four-lettered name of God, the *Yod* (י), *He* (ה), and *Vav* (ו), can also serve as suffixes for personal pronouns. Specifically, the suffix *Yod* means "me," *He* means "her," and *Vav* means "him."

Next, Kaplan explains that in the Hebrew alphabet, there are only two names to which these suffixes can be joined. These are the letters *Lamed* and *Bet*. Altogether, six Hebrew words can be spelled out.

1. *Li* לי to me

2. *Lah* לה to her

3. *Lo* לו to him

4. *Bi* בי in me

5. *Bah* בה in her

6. *Bo* בו in him.

Therefore, Kaplan writes

> The two letters, *Lamed* and *Bet*, are the only ones in the entire alphabet which combine with the letters of the divine name in this manner.[21]

---

20. Anonymous Hasidic work *Kitvei Qodesh*, 37.

21. Kaplan, *Sefer Yetzirah*, 9–10. See *Peliyah* 2d, Recanati, 18c, *Iggeret HaTiyul, Chelek HaSod* 2.

(20) Matityahu Glazerson (1937–)

Note: The first verse of the Torah contains precisely seven words and twenty-eight letters. According to tradition, the Torah was created for the sake of Israel. In addition, there is the well-known teaching that God, the nation of Israel, and the Torah are one (*Zohar* 2:73b). As a side note, that combination is found only in one other place in the entire Torah: the first verse the Decalogue (Exodus 20:1 "*God spoke all these words saying.*")

> *Torah, Light, and Healing*
>
> Creation with two "hands" is also hinted in the fact that the first verse of **Genesis** consists of twenty-eight letters. This verse contains seven words (corresponding to the seven days of Creation). The first three words contain fourteen letters (corresponding to one hand), and the remaining four words, fourteen letters (corresponding to the other hand).
>
> The verse that immediately precedes the Ten Commandments likewise consists of seven words and twenty-eight letters. The first four contain fourteen letters, and the remaining three, fourteen letters. This is a hint of the Sages' dictum that the world was created for the sake of the Torah, and on condition that Israel would accept the Torah (see Rashi to Genesis 1:1 and 1:31). It also hints that the Torah is the blueprint. It also hints that the Torah is the blueprint for Creation.[22]

(21) Fred Claar (1941–)

> "Israel means to struggle with God"
>
> In this week's portion, *Vayishlah*, Jacob wrestles all night with a mysterious angel representing God. Because Jacob successfully survives this encounter, his name is changed to Israel. The translation of Israel is "to struggle with God." The Torah is saying that to struggle with God is common. Most people require inquiry and study, as adults, to come to terms with their personal encounter. Jews are not asked to accept complete faith blindly. Jews are encouraged intellectually to encounter God within themselves after studying the wrestling our sages encountered in their journeys to God. It is possible to be a good Jew and have questions.[23]

22. Glazerson, *Torah, Light, and* Healing, 53–54. See Midrash Rabbah 1:1.
23. Claar, "Israel means to struggle with God."

(22) Rabbi Jonathan Sacks (1948–2020)

"Parshat Vayishlach in a Nutshell—The Core Idea"

After his wrestling match with the angel, Jacob was told: "*No longer shall you be called Jacob, but Israel,* for you have fought with God and men, and have won" (Bereishit 32:29). This new name is in fact given a second time in our parsha. After his meeting with Esau, and the story of Dina and Shechem, God tells Jacob to go to Beth El. Then we read: "After Jacob returned from Paddan Aram, God appeared to him again and blessed him. God said to him, 'Your name is Jacob, but *you will no longer be called Jacob*; your name will be Israel.' So He named him Israel" (Bereishit 35:9–10).

This is not an adjustment of an existing name by the change or addition of a letter, like when God changed Abram's name to Abraham, or Sarai's to Sarah. It is an entirely new name, as if to say that this will be a complete change of character. It is therefore puzzling that having said twice that his name will no longer be Jacob, *the Torah continues to call him Jacob.* God Himself does so. So do we, every time we pray to the God of Abraham, Isaac and Jacob. How can this be when the Torah twice tells us that his name will no longer be Jacob?

The Radak suggests that "*your name will no longer be called Jacob*" means, "your name will no longer *only* be called Jacob." You will have another name as well. This is clever, but it certainly is not the plain meaning of the verse. Sforno says, "In the Messianic Age, your name will no longer be called Jacob." This is also difficult. The future tense in the Torah generally means the near future, not the distant one, unless clearly specified.

A third approach is to read this not as a statement but as a request, a challenge, an invitation. Read it not as, "You *will* no longer be called Jacob but Israel." Instead read it as, "*Let* your name no longer be Jacob but Israel," meaning don't be what the name Jacob represents, rather be what the name Israel represents.

So the question is, what do the names Jacob and Israel represent?[24]

24. Rabbi Lord Jonathan Sacks, permission obtained from the Rabbi Sacks Legacy Trust. Rabbi Lord Jonathan Sacks, 'I Believe: A Weekly Reading of the Jewish Bible', on parshat Vayishlach, Koren Publishers, September 2022.

(23) Jeffrey Meiliken (1959 -)

"The Ultimate Reality Behind the Universe—Kabbalah Secrets."
Bereshit (בראשית) is the first word in the Torah. The root (ראש)
[*resh aleph sin*] of the word for first (ראשון [*rashon*, spelled *resh
aleph, sin, vav, nun*]) is in the heart of both *Bereshit* (בראשית)
and Israel (ישראל), last word.[25]

(24) Rabbi Aaron L. Raskin (1967–)

"*Yod*: The tenth letter of the Hebrew alphabet."
  Israel [ישראל] means both לי ראש [spelled *lamed yod—resh
alef sin*]—"I am the head," and שר א-ל [spelled *sin resh and alef-
lamed*] "minister of G-d." The terminology "minister of G-d"
represents the spiritual aspect of a Jew when he prays, studies Torah, performs acts of loving-kindness, and all the other *mitzvos*.[26]

(25) Rabbi Alex Israel (1967–)

"The Transformation of Yaakov."
  What is this new identity? At a basic level, it would seem
that his name is changed from Yaakov, the one who holds on to
the heels of others (see 25:26) to Yisrael, one *"who struggles with
God and man and prevails."* (32:28) Are we just being told that
Yaakov is now a "winner" rather than a "loser"? And has Yaakov
always been a loser? After all, he does succeed against Esav in
his struggle for the birthright and for the blessings although he
has to resort to a certain degree of deceit. Even with Lavan, he
succeeds against all odds, albeit using trickery.
  Maybe this leads us to a different assessment of the name
"Yisrael" as opposed to "Yaakov." The name Yaakov is not only
reminiscent of Yaakov's birth. It has a later meaning (27:36)—
that of trickery and underhand methods. In this sense, the
name Yisrael might come from the root YASHAR indicating a
more straight open approach. Not crooked but rather straight.
The twinning of these two verbs with this meaning is found in a

25. Meiliken, "The Ultimate Reality Behind the Universe."
26. Raskin, *Letters of Light*, 107.

passuk in Yishiyahu 40:4: "Vahaya haAKOV lemiSHOR—*And the crooked will become straightened.*"[27]

(26) Rabbi Danny Burkeman (1979-)

"The Pride of our Name."
    The word for 'wrestled' in the Hebrew text is
saritah

–

שרית [spelled *sin resh yod tav*].

While
saritah

–

שרית [spelled *sin resh yod tav*]
is part of the name Israel-
ישראל
it only appears in one other place in the whole of the Bible. When Hosea retells the story of Jacob, he uses the word to describe what happened: 'he wrestled with God and he wrestled with an angel'
(Hosea 12:4–5). What does it mean to wrestle with God? How can anyone wrestle with God? And how does Jacob emerge victorious after this wrestling match? The very name Israel is a constant reminder of this struggle.

When deciding on a name for the Jewish State, Israel was an appropriate choice. It is a name which we received as a communal title; we are called
    Bnei Yisrael
– the children of Israel. But more than just a name, it is a blessing which we received.

By blessing the Jewish State with the name Israel, the state became obligated to wrestle in two senses of the word. On the one hand, it was obliged to undertake a physical struggle, a fight to exist and survive—a clash which unfortunately Israel has been engaged with since its establishment. On the other hand, just as a person wrestles with their own conscience to always try to do the right thing, so too does the State of Israel seek to act according to its conscience, and be the best that it can be.[28]

27. Israel, "Shiur: Section III," lines 10–16.
28. Burkeman, "The Pride of our Name," #92.

(27) Boroch Fischlewitz (n.d.)

"Vayishlach"

Many of the commentaries deal with the question of why Yakov retained that name even after he was given the name Yisroel? The Malach of Essav [the angel of Esau] had just been defeated, but he would make one last attempt to prevail. He said (32:29) *"Lo Yakov Yeomar Ode Shimcha Ki Im Yisroel- No longer will it be said that your name is Yakov, but Yisroel."* The name Yakov equals 182, the name Yisroel equals 541. If we take away the name Yakov (182) from Yisroel we are left with 359 which is equal to Sotan [Satan]. However, if we keep the name Yakov in addition to Yisroel (Yakov V'Yisroel = 729) we have the numerical value of the words Kirah Soton—Eliminate Soton.

Alternately we need a Yakov plus a Sotan to reach Yisroel. As we say in Krias Shema: B'chol Livavecha—with all our heart means with both our drives. We must learn to love Hashem with both the Yetzer Tov and the Yetzer Horah. Without him there is no choice in the world. His true objective is to challenge us to fail so that we may overcome him and grow from the challenge.[29]

(28) Yeshem.com (2021)

"Shema Israel—Unity that Comes from Hearing—Kavanah for the word Israel"

The word Israel is composed of two words *Yashar El. Yashar* means straight and *El* means God at the level of *Binah* ["Understanding"]. Israel is therefore the straight path to God. This is the true meaning of the translation of Chosen People or *Am Segulah.*[30]

(29) Various Writers

"One Who Wrestles with God"

Known is that the name Israel [ישראל] means "one who wrestles with God" or "a God wrestler." Perhaps, Israel's name also alluded to an earlier wrestling match, when Jacob (whose

29. Fischlewitz, *"Vayishlach."*
30. Shema Israel, "Unity that Comes from Hearing."

name changes to Israel) was wrestling with his twin brother Esau while inside Rebekah's womb.

(30) Various Writers

Yisrael [ישראל] is the last word in the Torah [first in thought and last in action].

The last deed is first in thought (*Sof ma'aseh b'machshavah t'chilah*).[31]

(31) Various Writers

The words לי ראש [*li rosh*], "a head for me." = first in thought and last in action [Midrash Rabbah. In the beginning = for the sake of Israel = ישראל].[32]

Rabbi Zalman Baruch Melamed (1937–) head of the Bet El Yeshivah elaborates.

"In the beginning ('Bereshit') God created the heaven and the earth" (Genesis 1:1). "Bereshit"—The Sages interpret this as meaning "for the sake of 'the Beginning.'" i.e., "For the sake of Israel who are called 'the Beginning;' for the sake of the Torah which is called 'the Beginning,' etc." "For the sake of the Torah."— What do the Sages mean by "For the sake of Torah"? They mean that God created the universe in order that the Torah be fulfilled. It is also possible to understand this expression as implying that God made use of the Torah in creating the world. Indeed, the Sages teach that "God looked into the Torah and thus created the universe." They use an analogy of a person who wants to build a house, and proceeds to write up a blueprint according to which he will proceed. In the same manner, God looked into His blueprint—the Torah—and created the universe. No doubt,

31. This well-known saying is found in several Jewish sources. For example, in the song "*L'chah Dodi*," there is a stanza that reads, "Come, let us go to meet the Sabbath, for it is a source of blessing. From the very beginning, it was ordained; last in creation, first in God's plan." Furthermore, the first verse contains twenty-six Hebrew letters equal to the numerical value of YHVH. Only YHVH is the first and the last. Also see Stern, "'The First in Thought is the Last in Action'" *Journal of Semitic Studies*, 234–52. In addition, note that the first two letters of God's name Elohim (first thought), correspond to the last two letters of Israel.

32. *Midrash Rabbah Genesis* 1:5 reads, "R. Huna, reporting R. Jeremiah in the name of R. Samuel b. R. Isaac, said: The intention to create Israel preceded everything else." Also, see R. Abraham Ibn Ezra.

this analogy must not be understood literally, for God certainly does not need to write up and prepare blueprints.[33]

(32) Various Writers

Etymologically, the name Israel is derived partially from the word שר , meaning "master." It also is derived from the word *Yisra'* [ישרא spelled *yod sin resh aleph*] meaning to rule. Jacob wrestled with an "angel" and received a new name: Israel [ישראל]. Collectively, this hints that Jacob surrendered to God to be ruled by God.

33. Melamed, "For the Sake of the Beginning," lines 1–11.

6.

A *Sod* Analysis of Israel

6.1 CAVEAT

Sod DEALS WITH THE esoteric, mystical, and super-rational dimensions found in the Kabbalah. Readers are strongly encouraged to examine authoritative sources and standard references (encyclopedia entries). Noteworthy are the ten *sefirot* (Divine instruments through which everything came into being).

(1) Sefer Yetzirah Mishnayot 2:4–5 (ca. 200 BCE—ca. 200 CE).

> Twenty-two Foundational letters. He placed them in a circle like a wall with 231 gates. The Circle oscillates back and forth ... How? He permuted them, weighed them, and transformed them. *Aleph* with them all and all of them with *Aleph*; *Bet* with them all and all of them with *Bet*. They repeat in a cycle and exist in 231 gates. It comes out that all that is formed and all that is spoken emanates from one Name.[1]

Comment 1: Moshe Idel

Abraham Abulafia's Esotericism
Again using *gematria*, Abulafia calculates that the consonants of the Hebrew term for the Agent Intellect (*S´ekhel ha-Po'el*) are numerically identical to the noun *Yiśra' el*, since both phrases

1. Lancaster, "On the Relationship Between Cognitive," 243.

equal 541. The noun *Yiśra' el* is interpreted as being composed of *YeŠ* = 310, which means "there are," and *Ra' l*, the 231 combinations of two letters presented in some versions of *Sefer Yeṣirah.*[2]

Thus, *Aleph* and *Bet* are the first two letters of the Hebrew alphabet, and 231 is the number of two-letter combinations which may be generated from the 22 letters of the Hebrew alphabet, ignoring reversals.

Brain L. Lancaster writes, "Abulafia equates this wheel of the letters with the highest sphere of the intellect, seemingly the Active Intellect. Accordingly, the Active Intellect represents both the fount of ideas emanating into manifestation and the level of mind achieved through the successful practice of language mysticism. It is the sphere of union with the divine." He further elaborates

> In fact, this equivalence is established through the characteristic means of *gematria*, i.e., equating ideas through the numerical equivalence of phrases. *Yesh raʾel* ('There are 231' or 'Israel') = 541 = *sekhel ha-puʾal* ('Active Intellect'). *Gematria* depends on the fact that each Hebrew letter is also a number, *alef* = 1, *bet* = 2, etc.[3]

(2) Rabbi Bahya ben Asher (1255–1340)

Torah Commentary

Bereshit 32:29

"*for you have contended with Divine forces.*" In this instance the word *elohim* refers to the angel representing Esau with whom Yaakov had wrestled. The words *ve-im anashim* in the same line, refer to Lavan and Esau. According to *Bereshit Rabbah* 78,3 the words כי שרית עם אלוקים mean that Yaakov's countenance was engraved on the throne of G'd and the angel had realized this after looking at Yaakov . . .

Bereshit 32:30

A logical/investigative approach: The words: "*a man wrestled with him,*" refer to Gavriel. [We have shown on other occasions that Gavriel is referred to as איש "man." Ed.] According to the philosophers, Gavriel is symbolic of the active investigative intelligence. [According to Kabbalistic writings this disembodied intelligence supplies the outer form to human beings based

2. Idel, *Abraham Abulafia's Esotericism*, 181.

3. Lancaster, "On the Relationship," 243n12.

on their endowments (genes), Ed.] This force is the tenth of the emanations (the lowest counting from the top) the one we call מלכות [*Malkhut*] which is just one rung above the physical universe, the עולם העשיה [*Olam haAsiyah*]. This is the reason that the term איש which is usually only associated with tangible creatures is applied to Gavriel. Yaakov wanted to know if it is possible that this "man's" soul while still enclosed in a body could attain or represent a spiritual level equal to disembodied intelligences such as the force with whom he had done battle. [In other words, this category of angel might be perceived as the link between the highest intelligence found inside a body and the lowest intelligence able to exist as a disembodied entity. Ed.] The angel, i.e., Gavriel, answered him that this was possible only after dawn, i.e., until the various forces which darken the soul have disappeared with the light of morning. This physical light, though symbolic of spiritual light, is here described as עלות השחר [*Alot Hashachar* = Dawn].

Let me now explain the whole episode to you based on the premise we have just outlined. I am basing myself on a Jewish philosopher in Seville who wrote this commentary in the course of his discourse on Song of Songs. I have merely translated what he wrote into Hebrew ויותר יעקב לבדו, "Yaakov remained alone deep in thought, divesting himself of the influences exerted upon him by his body so that his thinking was unimpaired by such influences." He desired to know if his own intellect had attained the level which when the Torah speaks of certain celestial forces (such as Gavriel) is described as איש [man]. It is understood that what is described as התאבקות, "a wrestling match," takes place between evenly matched opponents. The Torah informs us here that in that struggle Yaakov did not attain superiority, i.e., the ability to function *just like* a disembodied spirit free from bodily influences, until the break of dawn. The word שחר stands for the restrictive influence of the body on the mind. Until Yaakov was able to rid himself of that influence, i.e., עד עלות השחר, "*until the departure of that* שחר*,*" he was not able to fully assert his שכל הפועל, his free-roaming intellect.

Now that the disembodied intellect no longer held an advantage over Yaakov's intellect, though the latter was imprisoned in a body, ויגע בכף ירך יעקב, and the forces of the body are identified by the expression כף ירך, the part of the physique which is essential in man, it became clear to Yaakov that his disadvantage vis-a-vis disembodied intellects was due only to the fact that he was imprisoned in a body.

At this point the disembodied intellect hints that the intellect embodied within Yaakov will become totally independent once the restrictive shackles of being imprisoned in a body, i.e., שחר are removed. The נפש השכלית, the intellectual life-force within Yaakov is on a par with the intellects of such disembodied beings as the angels. He (the "angel") mentioned this simile as something similar to someone who dismisses a servant or friend as he no longer needs him. It was a compliment the angel paid to Yaakov.

... this teaches that the intellectual life-force within Yaakov's body **held on** to the disembodied intellect represented by the "angel." He (Yaakov) was not prepared to let go of the disembodied spirit he had embraced during this nocturnal encounter until this force had left an imprint on him which would not become dispelled as soon as he released the disembodied intelligence from his "embrace." He insisted on attaining the intellectual level he had aspired to in an irreversible manner, not merely as a temporary spiritual-intellectual "high."

Remember that the name Yaakov has a connotation of "humiliation, degradation." We encounter this when he was born when the Torah described him as holding on to his twin brother's heel (Genesis 25, 26). Such an activity as holding on to someone else's heel is certainly creating an image of someone servile, someone in a degrading condition. After all, the heel is the very lowest part of the body. The name ישראל [Yisrael] by contrast evokes the image of something superior. This is why the "angel" said: "you are entitled to be known by a name which conveys something lofty." He gave as the reason for this change of name the fact that כי שרית עם אלו-הים ועם אנשים, that Yaakov's intellectual life-force had proven to be equal to the intellect of disembodied spiritual beings even though his own intellect was still imprisoned within a body. This is the meaning of the words אנשים ועם. Actually, there had been no need for this word; if someone holds his own in a contest with divine forces he is most certainly understood to be even to or superior to any human contestant. The use of the words עם אנשים therefore adds a new dimension to our verse. Yaakov was very anxious to have confirmation that his own נפש השכלית, was on a par with that of disembodied spiritual creatures though his own spirit was still connected to his body ...

I would add, based on the approach of this philosopher, that the fact that the Torah calls the name of the place where Yaakov had this encounter once פניאל [Peniel] and another time פנואל [Penuel] is a hint that the first name alludes to this angel representing the tenth emanation (meaning of the letter) י the type of angel known as איש. Once Yaakov/Israel had passed that place and had properly assimilated this new concept of man's נפש שכלית being capable of matching the spiritual level of the intellect of the disembodied angels, the place was called פנואל with the letter ו, as we now find that Yaakov was limping on his hip-socket. He had become aware of his body's being an impediment to spiritual progress which needed to be overcome. [Ed.][4]

(3) The Zohar (Moses De Leon, ca. 1240–1305)

Rabbi Hizkiyah opened, "It is written, *as a rose among thorns.*" (Song of Songs 2:2) What is the Rose? It is the Congregation of Israel. Because there is a rose, and there is a Rose. Just as the rose among the thorns is tinged with red and white, so is the Congregation of Israel affected by the qualities of Judgment and Mercy. Just as a rose has thirteen petals, the Assembly of Israel is surrounded on all sides by the thirteen attributes of Mercy. Thus, between the first mentions of the name Elohim, [in the Torah] these [thirteen] words surround and guard the Congregation of Israel.[5]

(4) The Zohar (Moses De Leon, ca. 1240–1305)

Parashah Yitro

When the Holy One, blessed be He, revealed Himself before Yisrael, He extended Mercy at first and afterwards He gave them the Torah, from the side of Gvurah, on the third day. THUS, THEY INCLUDE BOTH MERCY AND JUDGMENT,

4. Asher, *Midrash Rabbeinu Bachya*, 2:509–14. This well-known saying is in several Jewish sources. For example, in the song "*L'chah Dodi*," there is a stanza that reads, "Come, let us go to meet the Sabbath, for it is a source of blessing. From the very beginning it was ordained; last in creation, first in God's plan." Also see Stern, "'The First in Thought is the Last in Action'" *Journal of Semitic Studies*, 234–52. In addition, note that the first two letters of God's name Elohim (first thought) correspond to the last two letters of Israel.

5. Zohar 1:1a, Sefaria Community Translation. *The Zohar*, or *Book of Splendor*, is ascribed to Rabbi Simeon ben Yohai of the second century. However, academics state that Moses b. Shem Tov de Leon authored the text in the late 13th century. A variety of sources discuss this topic: Scholem, *Major Trends in Jewish Mysticism*, 156–204; Matt, *The Zohar*, Vol. 1. Also see Green's Introduction; *Encyclopedia Judaica*, 21:647–64 (an extensive bibliography).

as is appropriate for them. Hence, they are called 'Yisrael,'
FOR THE NAME 'YISRAEL' CONSTITUTES MERCY AND
JUDGMENT.[6]

(5) The Zohar (Moses De Leon, ca. 1240–1305)

Vayishlach: Verse 113

When Jacob saw this, he struck and overpowered him at dawn,
until he blessed him and confirmed to him the blessings, saying:
"Your name shall no more be called Jacob, but Yisrael" (Beresheet
32:29). THIS MEANS, YOUR NAME IS NO LONGER Jacob,
which indicates deceit—AS IT IS WRITTEN, "FOR HE HAS
SUPPLANTED (HEB. YA'AKVENI) ME THESE TWO TIMES"
(BERESHEET 27:36)—BUT YISRAEL, WHICH MEANS with
pride and might, for no one can prevail against you. FOR THE
NAME YISRAEL INDICATES PRIDE AND AUTHORITY,
AS IT IS WRITTEN, *"FOR YOU HAVE CONTENDED (HEB.
SARITA) WITH ELOHIM AND WITH MEN, AND HAVE
PREVAILED."*[7]

(6) Isaiah Horowitz (1565–1630)

Also known as the Shelah HaKaddosh, after the title of his best-known
work, Horowitz was a prominent rabbi holding several rabbinical positions
and was a kabbalist. *Toldot Adam* (*The Generations of Adam*), translated and
edited by Miles Krassen, presents a wealth of information for its readers.
One comment repeated in the literature relates to the numerical value of the
initial letters of the ten *sefirot*.

Toldot Adam
The House of Israel Gate [II]

The Shelah mentions that there exists an acronym formed by
the initial first letters of the names of the ten *sefirot* based on

---

6. Berg, *The Zohar: Yitro—Mishpatim*, 10:#287.

7. Berg, *The Zohar*: Vayishlach, 9: no. 113; Note: Tishby, *The Wisdom of the Zohar*,
3:1146n241, and n242 elaborates that "At night, when Judgment is dominant, the powers of *sitra ahra* are strengthened, but in the morning, when the light of *Hesed* shines,
the power of Jacob grows stronger." In addition, he further states, "The name "Jacob"
is derived from a verbal root denoting cunning, deceit. "Israel," however, is connected
with a root meaning "lordship, dominion."

gematria. Collectively, they total 541, as does the name Israel [20 + 8 + 2 + 3 + 3 + 400 + 50 + 5 + 10 + 40 = 541]. This meaning is established in Micah 2:13. *"The one who breaks through goes up before them; They break through, pass through the gate, and go out by it. So their king passes on before them, And the LORD at their head."* (NASB) The Shelah elaborates that the Hebrew word *r'osham* has the same *gematria* as Israel [*resh* (200) + *aleph* (1) + *sin* (300) + *mem* (40) = 541].[8]

(7) Rabbi Nathan Schapira (1606–1666)

Tuv Ha'aretz

The mystery of this is found in the passage in the *Zohar* talking about how *"Abba* is the Foundation of his daughter' (Pinchas 158a), which says that she is *Eretz Yisrael,* "*Yisrael Sabba.*" She includes ten levels to correspond to the ten nations, those levels are *keter, hokhmah, binah, gedula* (*chesed*), *gevurah, tiferet, netzach, hod, yesod* and *malkhut.* The first letters of those ten levels equal "Yisrael" [541] [ישראל). There in the midst of *Eretz Yisrael,* ten levels of holiness sanctify it.[9]

(8) Rabbi Moshe Chaim Ephraim of Sudylkov (1748–1800)

Degel Machaneh Ephraim, VeEthChanan (68d)

Paragraph 12: *And righteousness shall be for us . . .* And the crux of the matter is that when the Holy One Blessed Be He and may His Name Be Blessed creates His world, the world could not remain in existence for all things went back to their source and were in a state of *ex nihilo* until God created Israel and the world [fully] came into being and the name Israel itself guides us in this respect for the [letter] *resh* represents wisdom and the [letter] *lamed* represents understanding and the *aleph* represents knowledge.[10] And the letters ש"י contained in the word ישראל, the two letters that remain, are the essence of the existence and creation of the world, and existence (*Yesh,* יש) emanated from nothingness (*Ayin,* אין), and this is the essence of the name

8. Horowitz, *The Generation of Adam,* 160, 405.

9. Schapira, "*Tuv Ha'aretz.*" Note: 20 +8 + 2 +3 + 3 + 400 + 50 + 5 + 10 + 40 = 541.

10. *Resh* thus means "head," *lamed* means "learning," and *aleph* means "teaching" (Job 33:23). Cf. *Shabbath* 104a; *Pardes Rimonim* 27:15; 27:23.

Israel. And this is the crux of the existence of the worlds, where essence came from the void of nothingness, and therefore Israel is the fulfillment and completion of all worlds and of all creation. For without this, everything would retreat and go back to its primordial state of being—to the void of nothingness—and the essence inherent in Israel fulfills the essence [of being] of all the worlds, and that is when the Israelite man only has the internal essence only to allow the other worlds to exist and be fulfilled, to exclude someone who has too much of this essence, Heaven forfend. These words are both awesome and terrifying. And we must fully comprehend and take this to heart in ways which words cannot convey. And all of these words are able to be received based on the depth of the concept and the shortness of [comprehension] of the one who conceives these notions [mortal man] . . .[11]

(9) Harry Waton (1873–1959)

The Key to the Bible

The numerical value of these words

Take the words ישראל אלהי יהוה [YHVH *Elohai Ysrael*] Jehovah is the God of Israel, in the first aspect is 613. This number is well known: it symbolizes the Torah and its commandments. The commandments are supposed to be 613 in number [i.e., 248 positive and 365 negative commandments]. But this is of no significance; of significance is this: the commandments are identified with Jehovah the God of Israel.

יהוה 26 [YHVH]

אלהי 46 [*Aleph—lamed—he—yod*]

ישראל 541 [YSRAEL]

= 613[12]

(10) Rabbi Avraham Yaakov Finkel (1926–2016)

Introductory Material:

Midrash Rabbah—Genesis 12:15

---

11. Moshe Hayyim Ephraim of Sudylkov, *Degel Machaneh Ephraim, VeEthChanan* (68d).

12. Waton, *The Key to the Bible*, 48–49.

THE LORD GOD MADE EARTH AND HEAVEN [Why does the creation begin with the Divine Name *ELoHYM* as the Creator and end with two Names, *YHVH ELoHYM* when concluding the creation story? The Midrash explains:] This may be compared to a king who had some empty glasses. Said the king: 'If I pour hot water into them, they will burst; if cold, they will contract [and snap].' What then did the king do? He mixed hot and cold water and poured it into them. And so they remained [unbroken]. Even so, said the Holy One, blessed be He: 'If I create the world on the basis of mercy alone, its sins will be great; on the basis of judgment alone, the world cannot exist? Hence I will create it on the basis of judgment and mercy, and may it then stand. Hence the expression, THE LORD GOD.[13]

In My Flesh I See God: A Treasury of Rabbinic Insights about the Human Body

The prototype of the *Sefirah* of *Tiferet* is Jacob, the *bechir ha'avot*, "the favorite of the Patriarch," for he symbolizes truth, as it says, *"Grant truth to Jacob"* (Micah 7:20). Truth implies the proper mix of opposing attributes. Since *Tiferet* stands for the perfect blend of *Chesed* and *Gevurah*, it is fitting that Jacob is associated with this *Sefirah*.[14]

(11) Rabbi Aryeh Kaplan (1934–1983)

According to the early kabbalists 231 channels or heavenly gates exist to God. This number is derived from the Hebrew alphabet. It is through the Hebrew alphabet that God created the universe. *God said . . . and it was so* (e.g., Genesis 1:5, 6, 9, 14, 20, 24). Words are comprised of letters, just as compounds are comprised of elements. Therefore, metaphorically, the letters are likened to "spiritual elements" employed in creating the universe. Noteworthy, the Hebrew alphabet has twenty-two letters, and each combination of two letters makes up a unique "Heavenly gate."

Tzeruf or permutating is the act of combining. The number of combinations of twenty-two letters (two and two) without any permutation is calculated by a mathematical formula. Since there are twenty-two Hebrew letters, there are 21 x 22 = 462 possible permutations of the two-letter

---

13. Freedman, *Midrash Rabbah*, Genesis 12:15, 99. The Rabbis teach that the name *Adonai* (the Tetragrammaton) refers to God under His attribute of mercy. In contrast, the name *Elohim* describes Him as a God of judgment and severity.

14. Finkel, *In My Flesh I See God*, 53.

(biliteral) sub-roots. Given that each two-letter sub-root has two permutations, that are 1 x 2 = 2 permutations, there are 462 / 2 = 231 possible combinations.

The sages and kabbalists point out that the Hebrew word for a path is *"nativ."* The word is *nun* (50) *tav* (400) *yod* (10) *bet* (2), and significantly, it totals 462. In his commentary on *Sefer Yetzirah,* Kaplan devotes pages 113 to 123, with figures and tables elaborating on the significance of the number 231. These pages must be examined.

Significantly, Israel can access all of these gates. Kaplan and others write that this idea is "alluded to in Israel's name." That name can be rearranged into an anagram of יש רל"א, literally "there are 231 [gates]." Almost 1,500 years earlier, it was recorded in Midrash Rabbah 1:4 that at the beginning of creation, "Israel rose in thought." Therefore, "the name 'Israel' thus alludes to the fact that creation took place through these 231 Gates.[15] According to the later kabbalists, these 231 gates "are what remained in the Vacated Space that preceded creation." Kaplan provides numerous supporting sources.[16]

Kaplan continues writing

> When the author of Sefer Yetzirah speaks of the "32 Paths of Wisdom," it uses the word *Nativ* for "path." The numerical value of Nativ is 462, exactly twice 231. Since each of the 231 Gates contains two letters, there are a total of 462 letters in each array.[17] It is therefore evident that "Paths of Wisdom" are related to these arrays. In some versions of Sefer Yetzirah, the actual reading is "462 Gates."[18]

(12) Rabbi Arthur Green (1941–)

> Introduction." In *The Zohar: Pritzker Edition* 1
> The proper balance of *Hesed* and *Gevurah* results in the sixth *sefirah,* the center of the sefirotic universe. This configuration represents the personal God of biblical and rabbinic tradition.

---

15. Kaplan cites numerous examples found in the literature (364n46). *Ginat Egoz* 55b, *Otzar Chaim* 108a, *Perush HaNikkud* 48b, 49a, *Even HaShoham* 154a, 117b, *Tzaror HaChaim* (Jews College London, Ms. 318), p. 10a, *Gan Yah* 25b. See *Chayay Olam HaBah* 22b.

16. Kaplan cites *Emek HaMelekh* 6a, *Limudey Atzilut* (Munkatch, 1897), 3a, 22a; *Mikdash Melkh* on *Zohar* 1:16b, p. 31b, Rabbi Schneur Zalman of Liadi, *Likutey Torah,* Hosafot on *VaYikra* 53b. See chapter 1, note 32.

17. *Emek HaMelekh* 6b, *Limudey Azilut* 3a.

18. Kaplan, *Sefer Yetzirah,* 117–23, 363–64. He cites Donash, Barceloni, 208.

This is God seated on the throne, the one to whom prayer is most centrally addressed. Poised between "right" and "left" forces within divinity, the "blessed Holy One" is the key figure in a central column of *sefirot*, positioned directly below *Keter*, the divine that proceeds all duality. The sixth *sefirah* is represented by the third patriarch, Jacob, also called Israel—the perfect integration of the forces of Abraham and Isaac, the God who unites and balances love and fear.

Nonpersonal designations for this sixth *sefirah* include *Tif'eret* (Beauty, Splendor), *Rahamin* (Compassion), *mishpat* (balanced judgment), and *emet* (truth). The three consonants of *emet* represent the first, middle, and last letters of the alphabet. Truth is stretched forth across the whole of Being, joining the extremes of right and left, *Hesed* and *Gevurah*, into a single integrated personality. Thus is the sixth *sefirah* also described as the central "beam" in God's construction of the universe. Adopting a line from Moses' Tabernacle (Exodus 26:28), depicted by the rabbis as reflecting the cosmic structure, Jacob or the sixth *sefirah* is called "the central beam, reaching from one end unto the other."

In Jacob or *Tif'eret* we reach the synthesis that resolves the original tension between *Hesed* and *Gevurah*, the inner "right" and "left," love and judgment. The "blessed Holy One" as a personal God is also the uppermost manifestation called Israel," thus serving as a model of idealized human personality. Each member of the house of Israel partakes of this Godhead, who may also be understood as a totemic representation of His people below. "Jacob" is in this sense the perfect human—a new Adam, according to the sages—the radiant-faced elder extending blessing through the world. This is also the God of *imitation dei*. In balancing their own lives, the people of Israel imitate the God who stands at the center between right and left, balancing all the cosmic forces. That God knows them and sees Himself in them, meaning that the struggle to integrate love and judgment is not only the great human task, but also a reflection of the cosmic struggle. The inner structure of psychic life *is* the hidden structure of the universe; it is because of this that we can come to know God by the path of inward contemplation and true self-knowledge.[19]

---

19. Green, "Introduction," *The Zohar*, l.

(13) Rabbi Shmuel-Simcha Triester (1954–)

"The Source of All Blessing: When worthy, Israel draws the dew of blessing to the world"

Rabbi Yehuda was in the presence of Rebbe Shimon and asked him, "From what place do Israel receive a blessing?"

The *Mikdash Melech*, commenting on this question, says that "Israel" is the combination of two Hebrew words, *"li"* meaning "to me," and *"rosh,"* meaning "head," inferring that the People of Israel are the head to Gd, the first to receive blessing from the level of *Atzilut*.

Furthermore, he points out that the numerical value of 'Israel' is 541, the same as the first letters of each of the *s'firot*. This implies that Israel is a complete spiritual entity. Rabbi Yehuda is asking from which corresponding *s'fira* in *Atzilut* is blessing generated towards Israel . . .[20]

(14) Meiliken, Jeffrey (1959-)

The Ultimate Reality Behind the Universe—Kabbalah Secrets
The 7 Lower Worlds
While that is interesting, what is germane to our level of analysis lies in the details. The initials (אאאגנצת) of the 7 levels of superimposed prior Earth-like worlds sum to 546. This is just like the initials of the 10 *sefirot*/dimensions (כחבחגתנהים) that also sum to 546 and have a combined small *gematria* of 42.[21] It is also like the numerical value for Israel (ישראל) with the *kolel* for its 5 letters, 546.[22]

(15) Nissan Dovid Dubov (n.d.)

Discovering Jewish Mysticism: The Key to Kabbalah

20. Triester, "The Source of All Blessing." This text is from the teachings of Rabbi Shimon bar Yochai and based on the text *Metok MiDevash*. Readers should go to the Chabad website and examine the entire text.

21. *Kolel* refers to the number one being added for each of the letters of the word ישראל (i.e., five).

22. Meiliken, "The Ultimate Reality Behind the Universe." The seven worlds are: ארץ (*eretz*), Earth; אדמה (*adamah*), Ground; ארקא (*arqa*), Earth [Aramaic]; גיא (*gai*), Valley; ציה (*tsiyyah*), Dry Region; נשיה (*neshiyyah*), Oblivion; תבל (*tevel*), and Firm Land [or: World].

The *Sefer Yetzirah* speaks of 231 gates through which the world was created. This figure is arrived at simply by drawing a circle and writing the *Aleph Bet* around the circumference of the circle. If one now joined the *Aleph* and *Gimmel* with a line, and then with the *Dalet*, and so on with all the letters, you would have a total of 231 lines. The 231 lines connecting the 22 letters are called the "231 gates." This means simply that the gateway of creation is through the combination of letters that represent Divine powers. According to the early Kabbalists, the 231 gates are hinted at in the name "Israel." In Hebrew, Israel is spelled YiSRAeL. These letters can also spell out *YeSh RLA*, which literally means "there are 231," for the numerical value of the three letters *Resh, Lamed,* and *Aleph* equal 231. The *Midrash* states that at the beginning of creation, "Israel rose in thought." The name Israel thus alludes to the fact that creation took place through these 231 gates. Some Kabbalists identify these 231 gates with the letters of the residue (*Reshimu*) left after the *Tzimtzum*. [N.B. The number 231 represents the number of possible combinations of the twenty-two Hebrew letters in groups of two.][23]

(16) Several Sources

Gershom Scholem's article "Gematria," in *Encyclopedia Judaica* points out that another method of *gematria* is "The addition of the number of letters in the word to the numerical value of the word itself, or the addition of the number 'one' to the total numerical value of the word."[24] These methods are referred to as the *mispar misafi and kolel*. Several sources point out that the reality that Israel is a Godly nation can be derived from the fact that when the number five (i.e., the number one is added for each of the letters of the word 541 = ישראל] is added to its numerical equivalent [541], it equals 546.[25] In turn, 546 is the numerical equivalent of the sum of the first letters (initials) of the ten *sefirot*. Eliyahu Tougher elaborates that the number 546 is "the numerical equivalent of the word *Komas* (קמאת), which is also the numerical equivalent of the sum of the first letters of the ten *Sefiros* . . . This is referred to as *hagematria im ho'osios*."[26] (see table 9)

Table 9. The Sum of the Initials of the Ten Sefirot

23. Dubov, "Deeper Reality," 12th paragraph.

24. Scholem, "Gematria," 7:424–27, see 427.

25. Tougher citing Emden, *Siddur Yaakov Emden*, 44; Triester, "The Source of All Blessing," citing the *Mikdash Melech*.

26. Tougher, *Siddur Ha-Ya'avets*, 44n91.

Sefirot	Hebrew Letter	Name of the Hebrew Letter	Numerical Value
Keter	כ	*kaph*	20
Hokhmah	ח	*khet*	8
Binah	ב	*bet*	2
Chesed	ח	*khet*	8
Gevurah	ג	*gimel*	3
Tiferet	ת	*tav*	400
Netzach	נ	*nun*	50
Hod	ה	*he*	5
Yesod	י	*yod*	10
Malkhut	מ	*mem*	40
			546

(17) Several Sources

Originally, Israel was Jacob (Ya'avov), meaning heal. Rearranged, the letters of Israel form the words לי ראש, "a head for me." In other words, Israel has transformed from a heel to a head. In the language of the kabbalah, we have elevated ourselves from the lowest of *sefirot* (*Malkhut*) to *Keter* (the highest].

(18) Yosef Sebag (ca. 1973 –)

[Background information: The individual Jacob (Israel) corresponds to *Tiferet*, the sixth *sefirot*. The *gematria* of *Tiferet* is 1081. Significantly, the *gematria* of Israel (541) is the exact center point of 1081.] (See figure 2)

Star of David
Israel hints to a perfect/whole man—*Tiferet Yisrael* (the splendor of Israel).[27]

27. Yosef Sebag, "Star of David."

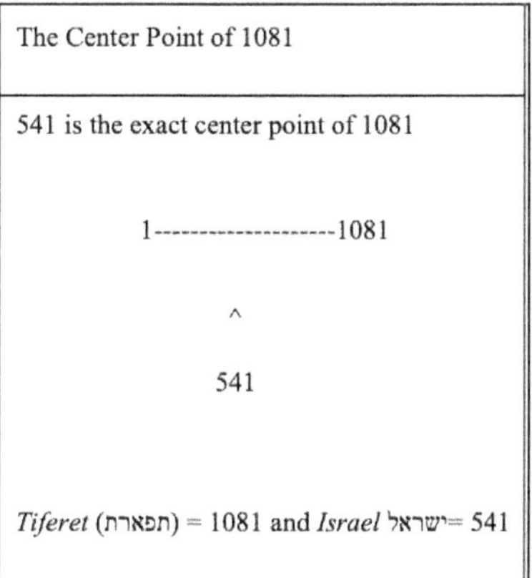

Figure 2. The Center Point of 1081

Rabbi Yitzchak Ginsburgh adds an interesting insight. He writes:

> At all levels all levels of Worlds, Souls, and Divinity, the number 100 represents perfection and completion . . .
>
> The word 'beauty,' יפי [*yode* or *yodah* = 10 + 80 + 10], itself equals 100. . .
>
> In the reduced numbering system, the sum of all 22 letters of the *alef-beit* is 100, 10^2. This is one of the secrets of the "ten intangible *sefirot* and 22 letters of foundation," the "32 pathways of wisdom" of *Sefer Yetzirah*. The sum of the first 10 letters from *alef* to *yud* is 46, the normative numerical value of the word מאה [*me-ah*], "one hundred." (46 equals לוי, Levi the "highest" of the tribes, while the remaining 54 equals דן, Dan, the "lowest" of the tribes.) The "triangle" of 46 (the sum of all the numbers from 1 to 46) is 1081, the *gematria of tiferet* (תפארת, consummate "beauty" and splendor).[28]

28. Ginsburgh, *The Hebrew Letters*, 293.

7.

New Age: The Number 2,701 and the Star of David

The Baal Shem Tov taught that nothing happens by chance; even if a leaf blows in the wind, it does so because God wills it.

7.1 INTRODUCTION

THE NUMBER 2,701 IS interrelated to Israel, the Star of David (i.e., the Magen David), the first verse of the Torah, and creation. An examination of the number 2,701 on the internet reveals numerous articles and blogs by Jewish and non-Jewish writers.[1] Several books also have sections analyzing and discussing the numerical value of Israel (541), the Star of David, and the first verse in the Torah.

7.2 THE NUMBER 2,701

The transliterated first verse of the Torah reads *Bereshit bara Elohim et ha-shamayim vet haʾaretz*. The total standard numerical value of these seven words and twenty-eight letters is 2,701 (see table 10).

---

1. Sebag, "Torah Numerology;" Evron, "Code of Creation;" Meiliken, "The Ultimate Reality Behind the Universe;" Duncan, "The 2012 Star Triangle Code;" Jenkins, "The Second Edge;" Park, "In the Beginning."

Table 10. The Total Numerical Value of the Torah's First Seven Words and
Twenty-Eight Letters

הארץ	ואת	השמים	את	אלהים	ברא	בראשית
haaretz	*vet*	*hashamayim*	*et*	*Elohim*	*bara*	*Bereshit*
296	407	395	401	86	203	913

Significantly, the number 2,701 is a *triangular number*. Like words, numbers conceal and reveal. A triangular number is displayable in dots or objects into a triangle. Furthermore, the pattern of dots arranges in an *equilateral triangle* with the same number of dots on each side (see figure 3). Notably, *the Star of David forms from two equilateral triangles.*

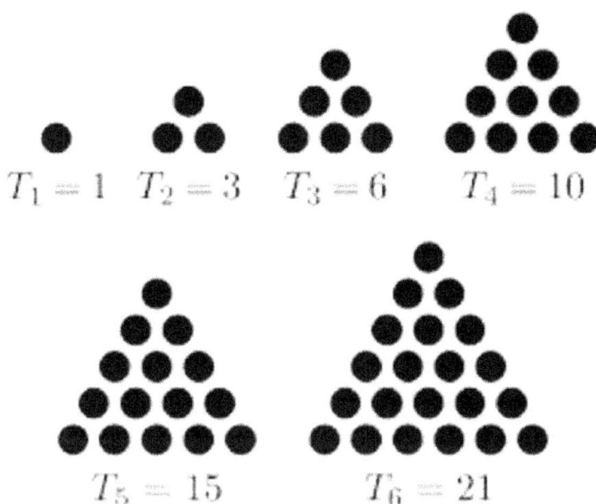

Figure 3. Triangular Numbers

Hence, the first triangular number is 1; the second is 3; the third is 6; the fourth is 10, the fifth is 15, and so forth. We can see that each triangle comes from the one before by adding a row of dots on the bottom. Consequently, it has *one more* dot than the previous bottom row. This relationship means that the *nth* triangular number *Tn* is equal to

$$Tn = 1 + 2 + 3 + \ldots + n.$$

The number 2,701 is the 73rd triangular number. Hence, $1 + 2 + 3 + 4 \ldots + 73 = 2{,}701$. The number seventy-three is conspicuous and intricately connected with Israel and the creation narrated in the Hebrew Bible. Most noteworthy, seventy-three is the *gematria* of the Hebrew word *Hokhmah.*

That word means "wisdom." In the *Zohar* (3:28a, 34a), *Hokhmah* reads as two words: *koach mah*, "the power or potentiality," or "the power of what is." For example, Psalm 104:24 says, "*Lord, how many are Your works! In wisdom [Hokhmah] You have made them all; The earth is full of Your possessions.*" (NASB) In some configurations (with the omission of *Keter*), it is the highest of the ten *sefirot*. The subject of *Hokhmah* is discussed extensively in the Kabbalah. Below, we will explore that number and others.

Now, let us look deeper into the number 2,701.

1. List of divisors: 1, 37, 73, and 2,701.

2. Prime factors: 37 and 73.

3. Therefore, the number 2,701 = 37*73.

4. Both prime factors (37 and 73) are mirror reflections [reflexive numbers of each other].

5. If we add 2,701 to its mirror reflection (i.e., 1,072): 2,701 = 37*73

    2,701 + 1072 = 3,773. Revealed in this sum are the original 37/73 prime factors. Besides, 2,701 is the 37th hexagonal number.

6. Both 37 and 73 are star (hexagram) numbers (discussed later).

7. The number 73 is the 37th odd number.

8. The number 73 is the 21st prime number. And, 21 X 21 = 441, the *gematria* of *emet* = Truth.

9. Interestingly, the digits of 2,701 add up to ten [2 + 7 + 0 + 1], as do the digits of Israel's *gematria*: 541 (5 + 4 + 1).

10. In addition, the number 45^2 (Adam = 45) + 26^2 [YHVH = 26] = 2,701.

Employing a mathematical analysis, investigators have uncovered several thought-provoking connections with the number 2,701. First, let us examine Israel's the letter expansion (*milui*) (see table 11).

Table 11. The Letter Expansion (*Milui*) of Israel Equals 2,701

Letters	*Milui*	Expansion	Numbers	Total
Yod (י)	[Yod-vav-dalet]	[Yod-vav-dalet] + [vav-aleph-vav] + [dalet + lamed + tav]	20 + 13 + 434	467
Sin (שׂ)	Sin-yod-nun	[Sin-yod-nun] + [yod-vav-dalet] + [nun-vav-nun]	360 + 20 +106	486

Resh (ר)	Resh-yod-sin	[Resh-yod-sin] + [yod-vav-dalet] + [sin-yod-nun]	510 + 20 + 360	890
Aleph (א)	Aleph-lamed-pe	[Aleph-lamed-pe] + [lamed-mem-dalet] = [pe-he]	111 + 74 + 80 + 5	270
Lamed (ל)	Lamed-mem-dalet	[Lamed-mem-dalet] + [mem-mem] = [dalet-lamed-tav]	74 + 80 + 434	588
Total				2,701

The result is precisely equal to 2,701. Therefore, Israel is connected intimately with creation.

Second, take each numerical value of the seven words of the first verse of the Torah and multiply them (see table 12).

Table 12. The Numerical Value of Genesis 1:1

הארץ	ואת	השמים	את	אלהים	ברא	בראשית
haaretz	vet	hashamayim	et	Elohim	bara	Bereshit
296	407 X	395 X	401 X	86 X	203 X	913 X

Thus: 913 X 203 X 86 X 395 X 407 X 296 = 304,153,525,784,175,760

Immediately following, add the *groups of thousands*. Adding these multiples, we obtain the numbers 304 + 153 + 525 + 784 + 175 + 760 = 2,701. Again, it bears repeating that these total equals Israel's letter expansion (*milui*).[2]

Third, once more, take each numerical value of the seven words of the first verse of the Torah and multiply them together. Thus: 913 X 203 X 86 X 401 X 395 X 407 X 296. Adding these multiples, we obtain the number: 304,153,525,784,175,760. Afterward, add the eighteen *digits* together.

3 + 0 + 4 + 1 + 5 + 3 + 5 + 2 + 5 + 7 + 8 + 4 + 1 + 7 + 5 + 7 + 6 + 0 = 73

The total number of seventy-three is precisely the triangular sum to obtain 2,701. [The number 2,701 is the 73rd triangular number, thus, 1 + 2 + 3 + 4 ... + 73 = 2,701.][3] Again, these total equals Israel's letter expansion (*milui*) and the value of *Hokhmah*.

2. Sebag, "Genesis and Pi;" Evron video.
3. Sebag, "Genesis and Pi;" Evron video.

Fourth, consider the following factoids discussed in Oren Evron's video, *Code of Creation: Part 1.*[4]

1. Calculate the reduced (small) *Mispar Katan* of the Torah's first verse (see table 13).

Table 13. The Total Numerical Value of the Torah's First Seven Words and Twenty-Eight Letters Using the *Mispar Katan*

הארץ	ואת	השמים	את	אלהים	ברא	בראשית
haaretz	*vet*	*hashamayim*	*et*	*Elohim*	*bara*	*Bereshit*
5 + 1 + 2 + 9 =	6 + 1 + 4 =	5 + 3 + 4 + 1 + 4 =	1 + 4 =	1 + 3 +5 +1 +4 =	2 + 2 + 1 =	2 + 2 + 1 + 3 + 1 + 4 =
17	11	17	5	14	5	13

Therefore, the *Mispar Katan* of the first verse is calculated by adding:

13 + 5 + 14 + 5 + 17 + 11 + 17 = 82

2. Multiply the number 82 (the *Mispar Katan* of the first verse) by the value of the words in that verse.

Thus, 913 X 203 X 86 X 395 X 407 X 296 X 82

The result is 24,940,589,114,302,412,320

3. Adding *each group of thousands* gives:

24 + 940 + 589 + 114 + 302 + 412 + 320 = 2,701. Thus, once more, this total equal Israel's letter expansion (*milui*).[5]

4. Multiply 24,940,589,114,302,412,320 by 82 (the *Mispar Katan* of the first verse).

The total = 2,045,128,307,372,797,810,240.

5. Now, *add each group of thousands.* The summation is as follows:

2 + 45 + 128 + 307 + 372 + 797 + 810 + 240 = 2,701[6]

6. Next, *add up all the digits* of 2,045,128,307,372,797,810,240

The result is 2 + 0 + 4 + 5 + 1 + 2 + 8 + 3+ 0 + 7 + 3 + 7 + 2 + 7 + 9 + 7 + 8 + 1 + 0 + 2 + 4 +0

This sum equals 82. It is the *Mispar Katan* of the Torah's first verse.[7]

Now examine the numbers seventy-three (73) and thirty-seven (37).

4. Sebag, "Genesis and Pi."

5. Sebag, "Genesis and Pi;" Evron video.

6. Sebag, "Genesis and Pi;" Evron video.

7. Sebag, "Genesis and Pi;" Evron video.

1. The number 73 is the triangular sum of 2,701.

2. The number 37 is the exact center point of 73 (see figure 4).

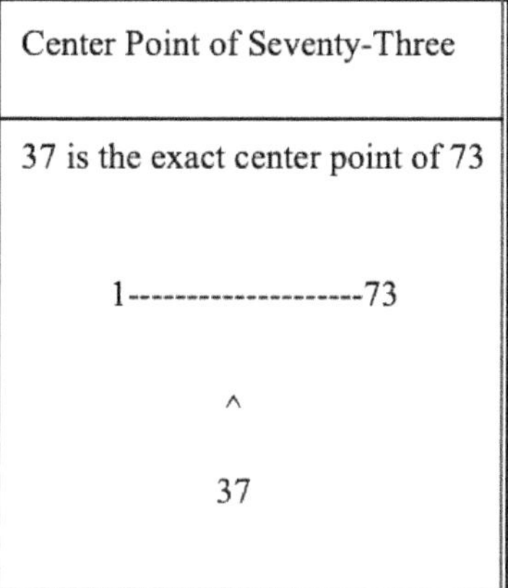

Figure 4. The Center Point of Seventy-Three

Furthermore, the standard numerical value of Genesis 1:1 = 37 × 73.

3. Calculating the Digital Root Sum of the Genesis 1:1 word value, we obtain:

913 (9 + 1 + 3 = 13 and 1 + 3 = 4)

203 (2 + 0 + 3 = 5)

86 (8 + 6 = 14 and 1 + 4 = 5)

401 (4 + 0 + 1 = 5)

395 (3 + 9 + 5 = 17 and 1 + 7 = 8)

407 (4 + 0 + 7 = 11 and 1 + 1 = 2)

296 (2 + 9 + 6 = 17 and 1 + 7 = 8)

or 4 + 5 + 5 + 5 + 8 + 2 + 8 = 37

Therefore, the digital root sum of the seven words of the first verse = thirty-seven (37), which is the mirror image of seventy-three (73).[8] In the ordinal system, the numerical value of *Hokhmah* is thirty-seven (see table 14).

Table 14. The Ordinal Value of *Hokhmah* Equals 37

ה	מ	כ	ח
5	13	11	8

In addition, the number 703 is noteworthy.

1. The *gematria* of the last two words (407 + 296) of the first sentence of the Torah total 703 (see table 15).

Table 15. The *Gematria* of the Last Two Words of Genesis 1:1

הארץ	ואת
haaretz	*vet*
296	407

2. The number 703 is the 37th triangle.

3. The number 703 is also the sum of thousands for 2,701 (2 + 701 = 703).

4. The number 703 is similar to 2,701 and 541. When adding their digits, the result is 10.

5. The number 703, like 2,701, is a triangular number.

How do the number 2,701 and the name of Israel interrelate with the Magen David (Star of David)? Before exploring this topic, we must briefly review the subject of a hexagram and triangular number. A *hexagram* is a six-pointed geometric star figure *formed by two equilateral triangles with the same center point and placed in opposite directions.* (See figure 5) The intersection is a regular hexagon. Significantly, and as discussed above, the number 2,701 is the numerical value of the first verse of the Torah and is the product of the triangular number: seventy-three (73).

Historically, the hexagon symbol is in *numerous* religions and cultures (e.g., Hinduism, Judaism, and Christian churches). Standard reference works (encyclopedias), Jewish organizations, and scholars, both Jewish and non-Jewish, admit that the seal of David [Star of David or, in the Hebrew, "*Magen David*" (literally, Shield of David)] is *not* a "religious" symbol in

8. Sebag, "Genesis and Pi;" Evon video.

any way (see figure 5).[9] Joshua Trachtenberg, author of *Jewish Magic and Superstition: A Study in Folk Religion,* says that "these figures are common property of humankind."[10]

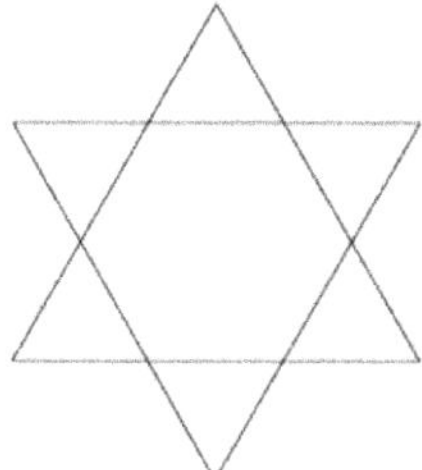

Figure 5. The Star of David

American Friends of Magen David Adom has an entry on the Star of David. They write the following words.

> Exact origins of the symbol's relation to Jewish identity are unknown. Several theories were put forward. According to one hypothesis, Star of David comprises two of the three letters in the name David. In its Hebrew spelling, it contains only three characters, two of which are "D" (or "Dalet," in Hebrew). In ancient times, this letter was written in a form much like a triangle, similar to the Greek letter "Delta" [(Δ)], with which it shares a sound and the same (4th) position in their respective alphabets, as it does with English. The symbol may have been a simple family crest formed by flipping and juxtaposing the two most prominent letters in the name.
>
> A popular folk etymology has it that the Star of David is literally modeled after the shield of the young Israelite warrior David (later to be King David). In order to save metal, the shield was not made of metal but of leather spanned across the simplest metal frame that would hold the round shield: two interlocking triangles. No reliable historical evidence for this etymology exists.[11]

The earliest known uses of the Star of David are decorative, including an excavated seal (sixth century BCE) and an arch dating back to the third or fourth century found on a synagogue in Galilee. Usage of a Shield

9. Bar Tzadok, "The Secret of David's Star & Solomon's Seal," 341–71; Israel Ministry of Foreign Affairs, "King Solomon's Seal"; Norman, *The Star of David*; Plaut, *The Magen David*; Reifmann, "Magen David"; Trugman, *Secrets of the Magen David*.

10. Trachtenberg, *Jewish Magic and Superstition*,141.

11. Delcau, "The Story of the Magen David," 9.

of David on a Jewish tombstone dates to the 3rd century CE in Taranto, Apulia, southern Italy. Employment of the hexagram in a Jewish context as a possible meaningful symbol may have occurred as early as the 11th century in decorating the carpet page of the famous Tanakh manuscript, the Leningrad Codex, dated 1008. It is the oldest surviving complete copy of the Masoretic text of the Bible. The earliest extant Jewish text to mention the hexagram (star) is the *Eshkol ha-Kofer* (ch. 242) by a Karaite, Judah ben Elijah Hadassi, from the mid-12th century.[12] He has seven shields used in an amulet for a mezuzah: "Seven names of angels precede the mezuzah: Michael, Gabriel, . . . Tetragrammaton protect you! And likewise, the sign, called 'David's shield,' is placed beside the name of each angel." The complete list of angels includes:

1. מיכאל (Michael)

2. גבריאל (Gavriel)

3. רפאל (Raphael)

4. ענאל (Anael)

5. שרמיאל (Sharmiel)

6. צדקיאל (Zedekiel)

7. אכחריאל (Akhariel)

By this century, the Star of David, as a Jewish amulet, was in use. A Tanakh manuscript, dated 1307, belonging to Rabbi Yosef bar Yehuda ben Marvas of Toledo, Spain, was decorated with a Shield of David.

Later, in the Kabbalah, the hexagram is seen. The *New World Encyclopedia* says:

> In medieval Judaism, popular Kabbalah made use of the Star of David, arranging the Ten Sephiroth, or spheres, in it, and placing it on amulets. Kabbalistically, the Star/Shield of David symbolizes the six directions of space plus the center, under the influence of the description of space found in the Sefer Yetsira: Up, Down, East, West, South, North, and Center. Congruently, under the influence of the *Zohar*, it represents the Six Sefirot of the Male (Zeir Anpin) united with the Seventh Sefirot of the Female (Nekuva).[13] However, the sign is nowhere to be found in

12. Hadassi, *Eshkol Ha-Kofer*, 92.

13. Scholem, "The Star of David," 262 says, "Max Grunwald, who has spun out many fantasies concerning this emblem, writes in 1923: 'This international sign was not accepted as a specifically Jewish symbol until Isaac Luria. He sees in it the image of the *adam kadmon* [the primeval man in the world of the divine ten spheres or *sefirot*]:

classical Kabbalistic texts themselves, such as the *Zohar* and the like Therefore, its use as a sefirotic diagram in amulets is more likely a reinterpretation of a preexisting magical symbol.[14]

The *New World Encyclopedia* adds the following insights.

> There are several interpretations of the meaning of the Star of David. Most frequently, the star is associated with the number seven (derived from the six points plus the center). This number has considerable religious significance in Judaism, which can be noted in several examples including the six days of Creation plus the seventh day of rest, as well as the Seven Archangels of God. In the same vein, the Star of David may have evolved as an abstract symbol of the Menorah (the more traditional symbol for Judaism that once stood in the Temple of Jerusalem), due to its association with light as well as its geometric organization into 3 + 3 + 1, which corresponds to the seven branches of the Menorah.[15]

Rabbi Naftali Silberberg writes from a kabbalistic perspective:

> The *Zohar* (3:73a) states, "There are three knots connecting [three entities] one to another: the Holy One, blessed be He; Torah; and Israel." The Jewish soul connects to its Creator through the study and observance of Torah. The triangle represents the connection between these three entities.[16]

In footnote 1, he elaborated: "The fact that in a triangle each of the three corners are connected to the two other ones demonstrates that the Jewish soul is itself knotted to G-d. Torah study and observance doesn't create a connection between the Jew and G-d—it merely brings it to light."

According to Gerbern S. Oegema,

> Isaac Luria provided the Shield of David with a further mystical meaning. In his book *Etz Chayim* he teaches that the elements of the Seder evening have to be placed in the order of

---

the six triangles plus the hexagon in the center represent the seven lower spheres while the upper three are to be conceived as lying above it.' . . . all these discussions were built on air." Grunwald's comment is available in his article "Jüdische Mystik" on page 392. It appeared in *Jahrbuch für Jüdische Volkskunde*.

14. *New World Encyclopedia* contributors, "Star of David," lines 37—42.

15. *New World Encyclopedia* contributors, "Star of David," lines 14—20.

16. Silberberg, "Star of David," lines 8—13.

the hexagram: above the three sefirot "Crown," "Wisdom," and "Insight," below the other seven.[17]

However, scholar Gershom Scholem strongly disagrees and refutes this (kabbalistic) view. He argued that Isaac Luria talked about parallel triangles, one beneath the other, and not the hexagram.[18] Additionally, Scholem opposed the opinions of many writers about the history and symbolism associated with the Magen David. In a sixteen-page English translated article, "The Star of David: History of a Symbol," he extensively challenged many beliefs.

> This subject of the shield of David seems problematic in every way. The scholarly and popular literature, which has dealt with it, consists of a chaos of assertions, some correct and others fantastic. Unfortunately, one cannot rely at all on previous writers, who mix their own, in part highly fanciful, explanations with the actual tradition of the Shield of David. Since they lack a clear idea of the real tradition, each one interprets it to his own liking. One says, We have before us a symbol of Judaism, i.e., of religious content and intellectual world of monotheism; another says: It is nothing but a symbol of Jewish "statehood" or "sovereignty," and just for this reason it deserves a place in the emblem of the State of Israel. One declares it is a distinctive mark of the wars of David's kingdom, the other considers it a symbol of harmony and eternal peace, the union of opposites and their neutralization in the principle of unity. All they have in common is the confusion they fall into when they try to prove an alleged traditional meaning for this symbol. They all get lost in idle talk and endless speculations which correspond to nothing in the particular symbol which invites mediation, and praised be he who has not locked the gates of association. . ..
>
> The hexagram is not a Jewish symbol, much less "the symbol of Judaism." None of the marks of a true symbol nor its manner of origin, described above apply to it. It expresses no "idea," awakens no primeval associations which have become entwined with the roots our experiences, and it does not spontaneously comprise any spiritual reality. It calls to mind nothing of biblical or rabbinical Judaism; it arouses no hopes . . . It does not appear at all in books on the religious life nor in the entire literature of Hasidism. And this was the case not because such meaning was

17. Oegema, *The History of the Shield of David.*
18. Scholem, *Hatakh ha-Zahav,* 156.

assumed and not considered problematical, but rather because no one even dreamt of such meaning.[19]

In contrast, Lilly Gelman writes in *Moment Magazine,*

> Steven Fine, a historian of Judaism in the Greco-Roman world at Yeshiva University, does not agree with either Scholem or Leet's claims: "We never know when things start, we just know what they look like later," he says. He cites French historian Marc Bloch's theory of the "idolatry of origins" that criticizes historians for focusing on the emergence of a symbol at the expense of studying its current meaning. "The real issue," he says, "is what does a living community do with it?"[20]

Galit Hasan-Rokem also criticized aspects of Scholem's essay. He pointed out that a 2011 Hebrew essay by Moshe Idel "reveals a rich treasury of magical uses for the six-pointed star in medieval Jewish sources, without claiming that the form has been adopted from some other culture."[21] He also "points to some biblical and Rabbinical sources empowering such uses . . ."

In the Hebrew context, the Star of David refers to the "Shield of David" (Magen David), a phrase first mentioned in the Babylonian Talmud, not as a symbol but as an epithet for God [*Pesachim* 117b].

In 1897, the First Zionist Congress adopted the symbol as its representation. David Wolffsohn (1856–1914), a well-known businessman in the early Zionist movement, wrote the following information.

> At the behest of our leader Herzl, I came to Basle to make preparations for the Zionist Congress. Among many other problems that occupied me then was one that contained something of the essence of the Jewish problem. What flag would we hang in the Congress Hall? Then an idea struck me. We have a flag—and it is blue and white. The Talith (prayer shawl) with which we wrap ourselves when we pray: that is our symbol. Let us take this Talith from its bag and unroll it before the eyes of Israel and the eyes of all nations. So I ordered a blue and white flag with the Shield of David painted upon it. That is how the national flag, that flew over Congress Hall, came into being.

19. Scholem, "The Star of David," 255–81, see 258–60. This essay was originally published in Hebrew (from the German *Almanach*) in 1948/49. Another English translation appears in *Commentary* 8 (1949) 243–51.

20. Gelman, "The Star of David," *Moment Magazine.*

21. Hasan-Rokem, "The Star of David and the Stars Outside," 78–89.

Naftali Nussenblatt (1895–1943) wrote an article about the Star of David as a symbol originally appearing in Yiddish in Vienna in *YIVO-Bleter*, 13 (1938), 460–76. ["Star of David, "Translator from Yiddish into Hebrew: Hava Eisenstein and translator from Hebrew into English: Ze'ev Barkan]. Two noteworthy excerpts we will highlight.

> At that time developed once again an argument over the Star of David. In the letter of sculptor Mark Antokolski to Stasov from 1879 we read: "as for a certain Gordon you mentioned in your letter to me, who attacks us that for our interpretation of the Star of David as a Jewish symbol, I am truly am amazed by the awkwardness of Mr. Gordon. Because according to my view it does not matter if it was a symbol of antiquity or not, and I would add in parentheses, for if the Star of David was created in the 14th century, more or less, it is impossible that it was created in King David's Time. for [*sic*] me it is enough that it existed for a long time, and that it is recieved [*sic*] by the people so ardently, as there are in every culture all sorts of possible legends, stories, traditions and symbols.
>
> In early political Zionism, the question was asked once again what sign will be used as its symbol. Herzl wrote in [his book] "The Jewish State" about a Jewish flag which has seven gold stars against seven hours of our working day. But various Zionist groups already used the Star of David as a sign and symbol. At first they painted the seven stars of Herzl around the Magen David."[22]

On November 30, 1896, Herzl met with Colonel Goldsmith in England. In Herzl's diary, he writes that Goldsmith "presented to me the flag of the Lovers of Zion: symbol of the twelve tribes." Later, in May 1898, Herzl detailed the Star of David question in correspondence with Dr. Max Bodenheimer. Afterward, he received a letter from him, which had a stamp that had a Star of David with 12 stars around it. [Herzl's letter to Max Bodenheimer 30.05.1898; Mai 1898, Welt 1910 Nr. 20, p. 472. Translation by Susanne Eisner-Kartagener] reads:

> One more thing. As a watermark you have used the shield of David, with a lion at its centre. So far we quite agree. However, here, in Romania, England, America the seven-pointed flag has already widely been accepted, with the following design:

22. During the Warsaw Ghetto uprising (April 1943), the Nazis captured Nussenblatt. He died in a concentration camp in November 1943.

> In my doodle the centre field is meant to represent a lion. In each of the six small triangles there is a star, as well as a star at the very crest. The twelve surrounding stars that you suggest are incorrect for the simple reason that the twelve tribes are already contained within the shield of David.

After the state of Israel's founding, the Star of David became part of its flag design, with *two equilateral triangles* forming a six-pointed star. The notice was published in the Official Gazette (*Reshumot*) no. 32, on 10 Heshvan 5709 (12th November 1948), page 2.):

> *The Provisional Council of State Proclamation of the Flag of the State of Israel*
> The Provisional Council of State hereby proclaims that the flag of the State of Israel shall be as illustrated and described below: The flag is 220 cm. long and 160 cm. wide. The background is white and on it are two stripes of dark sky-blue, 25 cm. broad, over the whole length of the flag, at a distance of 15 cm. from the top and from the bottom of the flag. In the middle of the white background, between the two blue stripes and at equal distance from each stripe is a Star of David, composed of six dark sky-blue stripes, 5.5 cm. broad, which form two equilateral triangles, the bases of which are parallel to the two horizontal stripes.
> 25 Tishrei 5709 (28 October 1948)
> Provisional Council of State
> Joseph Sprinzak, Speaker

Alec Mishory, art historian, critic, and lecturer at the Open University, wrote these words.

> Zionist tradition credits the design of the Zionist flag to David Wolffsohn. Legend even tells precisely when Wolffsohn had his brainstorm, namely, that during a meeting in Basel Herzl raised the question of the Zionist flag. When his proposal of a white banner with seven gold stars failed to marshal a consensus, Wolffsohn stood up and said: "Why do we have to search? Here is our national flag." Upon which he displayed his prayer shawl and showed everyone the national flag: a white field with blue stripes along the margin. In our attempt to uncover the message conveyed by the Zionist flag, we should therefore address each of its components separately—the Magen David (Star of David), the blue stripes and the white background.[23] (see figure 6)

23. Mishory, "The Flag and the Emblem."

Figure 6. The Flag of Israel

Now, let us examine additional "New Age" insights.

First, the *gematria* of the name Israel is 541. That number is noteworthy. It is a "Star Number."

1. A star number is a centered figurate number, a centered hexagram (six-pointed star), such as Chinese checkers. The nth star number calculation is the formula $Sn=6*n*(n-1)+1Sn=6*n*(n-1)+1$. The first 43-star numbers are:

   1, 13, 37, 73, 121, 181, 253, 337, 433, *541*, 661, 793, 937, 1093, 1261, 1441, 1633, 1837, 2053, 2281, 2521, 2773, 3037, 3313, 3601, 3901, 4213, 4537, 4873, 5221, 5581, 5953, 6337, 6733, 7141, 7561, 7993, 8437, 8893, 9361, 9841, 10333, 10837 (sequence A003154 in the OEIS).

2. The number 541 is not only a star number but a prime number.

3. Moreover, 541 is the 100th prime number.

4. Furthermore, 541 is the 10th hexagonal star number whose figure is a six-pointed star like the Star of David (the symbol for the flag of Israel). Also notable, the number ten coincides with the numerical value of the first letter of the Tetragrammaton and the name Israel.

The mathematical formula for "Star of David" (Hexagram) figurate numbers is $Star(n) = 6n(n-1)+1$ (see table 16). A figurate number is a number capable of being represented by a regular geometrical arrangement of equidistant points.

Table 16. The Mathematical Formula for "Star of David" (Hexagram)

1	$6^*1(1-1)+1$	=	1
2	$6^*2(2-1)+1$	=	13
3	$6^*3(3-1)+1$	=	37
4	$6^*4(4-1)+1$	=	73
5	$6^*5(5-1)+1$	=	121
6	$6^*6(6-1)+1$	=	181
7	$6^*7(7-1)+1$	=	253
8	$6^*8(8-1)+1$	=	337
9	$6^*9(9-1)+1$	=	433
10	$6^*10(10-1)+1$	=	541

Hexagon/Star pairs (e.g., 541) are closely related to triangular numbers (e.g., 2,701). Their product is always a triangle, which can be generated symmetrically from a pair of triangles.

The question that begs inquiring is whether there is a sign that the Hebrew word "Israel" (ישראל) and the "Star of David" figurate are mathematically connected. What we know is

1. 2,701 is the 73rd Triangular Number T(73) and equals 37 x 73.

2. Sum of *Bereshit* /Genesis 1:1 = 2,701 = 37 x 73 = T(73).

3. The *milui* value of Israel is 2,701.

4. Both 37 and 73 are star numbers. They are geometrically related to each other as being a hexagon/star pair, as shown below.

5. The Star of David is "formed by two equilateral triangles (hexagram) which have the same center point and placed in opposite directions."

7.3. ADDITIONAL CONSIDERATIONS

Eighty is the *gematria* of the Hebrew letter *pe*, which means "mouth" in Hebrew. In contrast, twenty-six is the *gematria* of God's Name—the Tetragrammaton: YHVH [10 + 5 + 6 + 5 = 26].

The Master kabbalist Rabbi Moshe Hayyim Luzzato wrote:

> And on this it is written: "*For the L-ORD gives wisdom, out of His mouth comes knowledge and understanding*" (Mishlei 2:6). For all that exists is from the word of the Holy One blessed be He. Because this "mouth" (of G-d) is the root of all creations, and this itself sustains their existence. And the "*hevel*" (breath), which means the *hashpaah* (influence, energy) which goes out to all creations form the source which took it out. And therefore it is written "*that man does not live by bread only, but by everything that goes out of the mouth of the L-ORD does man live*" (Devarim 8:3), which is this "*hevel*" which goes out and sustains . . ." (*Derech Etz Chaim*, par. 8).

Interestingly, the Hebrew word "*hevel*," which means "breath," has the *gematria* of thirty-seven (37). *Hevel* (in various forms) has exactly seventy-three (73) occurrences in the Tanakh.[24] Appendix 6 identifies those occurrences. In addition, *hevel* occurs thirty-seven times in the book of Ecclesiastes (*Koheleth/Qoheleth*). As previously mentioned, Genesis 1:1 has a *gematria* value of 2,701 = 37*73.

---

24. See. https://biblehub.com/hebrew/strongs_1892.htm

8.

Contraction

There are approximately 150 insights from the literature in this compendium on interpreting the name Israel. The material spans over two millennia, many locales, and numerous cultures. Following is a condensed presentation.

8.1. PUTTING IT ALL TOGETHER

1. Israel is the divine name given by God (Genesis 35: 10–11) that identifies with a

    a. distinct person, Jacob,

    b. distinct people, the children of Jacob/Israel, and the assembly or congregation of Israel,

    c. distinct nation, and

    d. a distinct piece of land: the Holy Land.

2. The divine title *K'lal Ysrael* ("assembly or congregation of Israel") has a numerical value of 676. The Tetragrammaton squared (26 X 26) totals 676.

3. The divine name Israel [ישראל] is an anagram for the three patriarchs (Abraham, Isaac, and Jacob) and four matriarchs (Sarah, Rachel, Rebekah, and Leah). Therefore, the name of Israel contains the Jewish people's spiritual DNA.

4. The divine name Israel [ישראל] is an anagram "*Yesh Shishim Ribo Osiyo LaTorah*" ("there are sixty myriads [=600,000] of letters in the Torah")

5. The divine partnership in the product of Israel is concealed within that divine name. The numerical value of Israel [(ישראל)] is 541 [10 + 300 + 200 + 1 +30]. The number 541 is the product of Jacob's father Isaac (יצחק = *yod tsade khet pe,* 208) + his mother Rebekah (307 = רבקה = *resh bet qoph he*) + YHVH (26 = יהוה).

6. The sum of Rebekah is 307 and Jacob 182, to which one adds 52, which is 2 x YHVH, and the sum of all four is 541.

7. The fact that Israel (ישראל) is a Godly nation is derivable from the fact that when the number five is added to its numerical equivalent since there are five Hebrew letters in the word Israel. Five added to 541 totals 546. This number equals the numerical equivalent of the word *Komas* (קומת) [spelled *qoph vav mem tav* = 100 + 6 + 40 + 400 = 546], which is also the numerical equivalent of the sum of the first letters of the ten *sefirot*: *Keter, Hokhmah, Binah, Chesed, Gevurah, Tiferet, Netzach, Hod, Yesod,* and *Malkhut.* Through the *sefirot,* God created the universe.

8. If the numerical values of the two names of God—אהיה [*Ehyeh*] (1 + 5 + 10 + 5 + 2 = 21) and יהוה [YHVH] (10 + 5 + 6 + 5)—Are multiplied together (21 X 26 = 546), the total equals the numerical value of ישראל (Israel = 10 + 300 + 200 + 1 + 30 = 541) plus the number (5) of the word's letters (541 + 5 = 546)

9. The name Jacob equals 182, and Israel equals 541. Jacob received an additional name Israel after he wrestled the stranger (Satan = 359). Adding the numerical values of Jacob (182) with Satan (359) precisely equals the *gematria* for Israel (541).

10. The divine means of Israel's redemption from Egyptian bondage is concealed in its name. The standard *gematria* value of the Ten Plague's eleven (11) initials add up to 541 (when employing two initials for the last plague). That number, 541, is also the *gematria* for the name Israel.

11. The number 541 of Israel corresponds to the *sekhel ha-po'el,* the Active Intellect through which one connects with God.

12. The number 541 of Israel also corresponds to the *gematria* of the *mitzvot* (*haMitzvot* = 541).

13. The numerical value of the last letters of the words: *"Kol Yisrael yeish lahem cheilek le'Olam Haba"* — "All Israel have a share in the World to Come" is five hundred and forty-one (541), which is also the numerical value of the word *"Yisrael"*

14. Israel corresponds to *Tiferet*, the sixth of the *sefirot*. *Tiferet* means beauty. In addition, the number 541 is the exact midpoint of 1081—the numerical value of *Tiferet*.

15. The word beauty, יפי [*yafah* [male] or *yofe* [female] spelled *yod pe yod*] equals 100 (= 10^2), and in the reduced numbering system, all of the letters of the Hebrew *aleph-bet* are 100. Furthermore, the sum of the first ten letters from *aleph* to *yod* is 46, the normative numerical value of the word מאה [*me-ah; spelled mem aleph he*], "one hundred." Interestingly, the "triangle" of 46 (the sum of all the numbers from 1 to 46) is 1081, the *gematria* of *Tiferet* (תפארת, consummate "beauty" and splendor).

16. The first letter of the Torah is an enlarged *bet* for the word *Bereshit*. The white space inside the *bet* forms the pregnant letter *pe*, meaning mouth.

    a. The letter *pe* resembles a mouth with a tooth emerging from its upper jaw.

    b. There are thirty-two teeth in an adult.

    c. God's name appears thirty-two times in the creation narratives (Genesis 1:1–2:3). Also, this number parallels the numerical value of the Torah's first (*bet*) and last (*lamed*) letters (2 + 30).

    d. The full spelling of the letter *pe* is *pe aleph*. These two letters split *into yod vav vav yod*, as explained by the Arizal: sixteen (*yod vav*) from above and sixteen (*yod vav*) from below, in correspondence to the thirty-two teeth, which all derive from the secret of: " . . . *and I will teach you wisdom* (Job 33:33)." (NASB) (*Siddur HaArizal*, beginning of the *Amidah*.)

    e. How does the Torah describe God's means of creation? Metaphorically (The Torah speaks in the language of man.), the answer is God speaks (*va'Yomer*) "through the mouth of space.

        1. Psalm 33:6 *By the word of the LORD the heavens were made,*

        2. *And by the breath of His mouth all their lights.* (NASB)

        3. Psalm 33:9 *For He spoke, and it was done; He commanded, and it stood firm.* (NASB)

        4. Psalm 148:5 *They are to praise the name of the Lord, For He commanded and they were created.* (NASB)

8.2. THE FIRST WORD OF THE TORAH AND THE CREATION PROCESS: BERESHIT

Often, *Bereshit* is translated "In the beginning" or "In the beginning of."[1] In addition to speech, the Hebrew Bible offers other insights into the creation process.

1. Jeremiah 10:12 *It is He who made the earth by His power, Who established the world by His wisdom; And by His understanding He has stretched out the heavens.* (NASB)

2. Jeremiah 51:15 *It is He who made the earth by His power, Who established the world by His wisdom, And by His understanding He stretched out the heavens.* (NASB)

3. Proverbs 3:19 *The LORD founded the earth by wisdom, He established the heavens by understanding.* (NASB)

4. Proverbs 8:22 *The LORD created me [i.e., Wisdom] at the beginning of His way, Before His works of old.* (NASB)

The word "beginning" refers to *Hokhmah*, which is wisdom. Here, the Sages interpret the phrase "*reishit Hokhmah*," which can poetically mean "the beginning is wisdom." Interestingly, the first word of the Torah, *Bereshit*, translates, "In the beginning (God created the heavens and the earth)." The Targum Yonatan translates it as, "With *Hokhmah* (God created . . .)." As will soon become apparent, the concept of *Hokhmah*, that is, "wisdom," is intimately connected with the first verse of the Torah and specifically the name Israel. First, some necessary background facts.

1. The first verse consists of seven words and twenty-eight letters.

2. It is noteworthy that a combination of seven words and twenty-eight letters in one verse occurs *only* one other time in the Hebrew Bible: Exodus 20:1. That is the first verse of the Decalogue (the Ten Commandments) that begins with the word: *Anochi.*

3. The number twenty-eight (corresponding to the number of letters in the first verse of the Bible) is significant in that it is a perfect number and a triangular number. A perfect number is a positive integer equal to the sum of its proper divisor. The number twenty-eight is perfect because 14, 7, 4, 2, and 1 add up to 28. It is also a triangular number because the sum of the numbers equals itself: $1 + 2 + 3 + 4 + 5 + 6 + 7 =$

---

1. David Sheinkin, in *Path of the Kabbalah*, discusses twelve possible translations of the opening line of Genesis, 51–56.

28 (triangular sum). Additionally, the first word of the Torah, *Bereshit*, is composed of six Hebrew letters. The number six is also perfect and triangular: 1 + 2 + 3 = 6.

4. Noteworthy, the numerical value of the first verse in the Hebrew Bible is 2,701, which is the 73rd triangular number. Thus, 1 + 2 + 3 + 4 + . . . + 73 = 2,701.

5. Moreover, the word *hokhmah* (i.e., "Wisdom") has a numerical value of seventy-three. In the Ordinal system, it becomes thirty-seven.

6. Consequently, concealed in the first verse is the *means* of creation: wisdom.

7. Last, the number thirty-seven is the exact center point of seventy-three.

8.3. FACTS RELATED TO THE NUMBERS 2,701, 73, AND 541

1. The numerical value of the first verse in the Bible is 2,701.

2. The list of divisors of 2,701 are 1, 37, 73, and 2,701. Its prime factors are 37 and 73.

3. Therefore: 2,701 = 37*73

4. Both prime factors (37 and 73) are mirror reflections [reflexive numbers] of each other.

5. The number 37 is the 12th prime number, 73 is the 21st prime number, and these order numbers 12—21 are also decimal reflections [reflexive numbers].

6. The word *hokhmah*, "Wisdom," has an ordinal numerical value of thirty-seven.

7. If we add 2,701 to its mirror reflection: 2,701 + 1,072 = 3,773. Notice that the original 37/73 prime factors are revealed in this sum.

8. Therefore, the number 3,773 is a palindrome that reads the same, forwards and backward.

9. The number 2,701 is also the 37th hexagonal number.

10. Both thirty-seven and seventy-three, too, are star (hexagram) numbers.

11. The number seventy-three is the 37th odd number.

12. The number seventy-three is the triangular sum of 2,701.

13. The number thirty-seven is the exact center point of seventy-three.

14. The number 45^2 (Adam = 45) + 26^2 [YHVH = 26) = 2,701.

15. The relationship to the name Israel: The multiple of the *gematria* of the seven words of the Torah's first verse together totals: 304,153,525,784,175,760 and the Sum of the Thousands: 304 + 153 + 525 + 784 + 175 + 760 = 2,701. In turn, the expanded numerical value of Israel totals 2,701.

16. The Letter Expansion (*milui*) value of Israel is 2,701.

17. Adding the eighteen *digits* together of 3 + 0 + 4 + 1 + 5 + 3 + 5 + 2 + 5 + 7 + 8 + 4 + 1 + 7 + 5 + 7 + 6 + 0 = 73.

18. The first verse consists of seven words and twenty-eight letters. It is noteworthy that a combination of seven words and twenty-eight letters in one verse occurs *only* one other time in the Hebrew Bible: Exodus 20:1. That is the first verse of the Decalogue (the Ten Commandments) that begins with the word: *Anochi*.

19. The number twenty-eight (corresponding to the number of letters in the first verse of the Bible) is significant in that it is a perfect number and a triangular number. A perfect number is a positive integer equal to the sum of its proper divisor. The number twenty-eight is perfect because 14, 7, 4, 2, and 1 add up to 28. It is also a triangular number because the sum of the numbers equals itself: 1 + 2 + 3 + 4 +5 + 6 +7 = 28 (triangular sum). Additionally, the first word of the Torah, *Bereshit*, is composed of six Hebrew letters. The number six is also a perfect and triangular: 1 + 2 + 3 = 6.

20. Noteworthy, the numerical value of the first verse in the Hebrew Bible is 2,701, which is the 73rd triangular number. Thus, 1 + 2 + 3 + 4 + . . . + 73 = 2,701.

21. Moreover, the word *hokhmah* (i.e., "Wisdom") has a numerical value of seventy-three. In the Ordinal system, it becomes thirty-seven.

22. Consequently, concealed in the first verse is the *means* of creation: wisdom.

23. The number 541 is a "Star Number":

   a. A star number is a centered figurate number, a centered hexagram (six-pointed star), such as one played with Chinese checkers. The nth star number calculation is the formula Sn=6∗n∗(n−1)+1Sn=6∗n∗(n−1)+1.

   b. The number 541 is not only a star number but a prime number.

c. Moreover, 541 is the 100th prime number.

d. Furthermore, 541 is the 10th hexagonal star number whose figure is a six-pointed star like the Star of David (the symbol for the flag of Israel). Notable, the number ten coincides with the numerical value of the first letter of the Tetragrammaton and the name Israel.

e. The individual Jacob (Israel) corresponds to *Tiferet,* the sixth *sefirot.* The *gematria* of *Tiferet* is 1081. Significantly, the *gematria* of Israel (541) is the exact center point of 1081.

8.4. THE RELATIONSHIP TO ISRAEL: "THE END OF THE ACTION WAS AT FIRST IN THOUGHT" (*SOF MA'ASEH B'MACHSHAVAH T'CHILAH*)

1. *Bereshit* is the first word of the Torah. Frequently, it is defined "In the beginning" or "In the beginning of." In contrast, the last word in the Torah is "Israel." *Sof ma'aseh b'machshavah t'chilah* alludes to the idea that "in the beginning was Israel."

2. If the six letters of the first word of the Torah [*Bereshit*] are rearranged, we obtain the words ראש לי, [*li rosh= lamed yod and resh aleph shin*] meaning "a head for me." This idea also corresponds with the dictum "first in thought and last in action [midrash: In the beginning = for the sake of Israel = ישראל Israel].

3. *Bereshit* (בראשית) is the first word in the Torah: The root (ראש) (*resh aleph shin*) of the word for "first" (ראשון) [*rishon = resh aleph shin vav nun*]) is in the heart of both *Bereshit* (בראשית) and Israel (ישראל), the last word.

4. Deuteronomy 7:6 *For you are a holy people to the Lord your God; the Lord your God has chosen you to be a people for His personal possession out of all the peoples who are on the face of the earth.* (NASB) [This passage substantiates the opinion that metaphorically speaking, Israel was "first" in God's thoughts.]

5. Deuteronomy 14:2 *For you are a holy people to the Lord your God, and the Lord has chosen you to be a people for His personal possession out of all the peoples who are on the face of the earth.* (NASB) [Similarly, this passage corroborates the idea that, metaphorically speaking, Israel was "first" in God's thoughts.]

8.5. UNIQUE FEATURES (AND HINTS) OF THE LETTERS FORMING THE NAME ISRAEL

1. A *yod* is the first letter of the Tetragrammaton (YHVH). The *yod* is thus employed, representing God's name. The letter *yod* also represents the single point that all of the Creator's creation emerges and the Unity of multiplicity. Moreover, the number ten symbolizes completion, unity, holiness, and sanctity. The *yod* is also the first letter in the name Israel.

2. The letter *lamed*, the last letter in Israel, is formed out of a *kaph* (כ): the number twenty, and a *vav* (ו), the number six. Together, they total twenty-six, equivalent to the Tetragrammaton, YHVH [10 + 5 + 6 + 5] equals twenty-six.

3. Within the name of Israel, the divinity of God is concealed. In effect, the first and last letters are divine-like bookends.

4. Israel contains the Hebrew alphabet's smallest (*yod*) and tallest (*lamed*) letters.

    a. The small *yod* implies that when Israel is humble, God is immanent. In contrast, when Israel is arrogant, as symbolized by the tall *lamed*, God is transient.

    b. One has the potential to develop from a small child (the small *yod*) into a great person or even a great scholar (the tall *lamed*).

5. The shape of the letter *lamed*.

    a. The *yod* looks like a flame that soars ever higher, representing the soul of a Jew yearning to unite with God.

    b. The *lamed* [ל] hints that people should strive upward to connect with God.

6. The Vowels of the Letters

    a. The sum numerical value of the four lowest vowels in Israel: *hireq* (10), *shewa* (20), *qamets* (16), and *tsere* (20), is sixty-six (66). Genesis 46:26 reports, "*All the people belonging to Jacob, who came to Egypt, his direct descendants, not including the wives of Jacob's sons, were sixty-six persons in all.*" (NASB)

    b. In contrast (subject to speculation), the sum numerical value of all five vowels in Israel: *hireq* (10), *shewa* (20), *holam* (10), *qamets* (16), and *tsere* (20) totals seventy-six (76). In *gematria* (*mispar katan*), seven plus six equals thirteen. That number coincides with Israel's total number of male and female children.

8.6. THE STAR OF DAVID (MAGEN DAVID)

The Star of David (Magen David) is a six-pointed star (hexagram). It is formed by two equilateral triangles with the same center point and placed in opposite directions. Noteworthy

1. A triangular number forms an equilateral triangle.

2. The number 2,701 is the 73rd triangular number and it is intimately connected with creation and Israel.

3. The letter expansion of Israel (*Milui*) equals 2,701 and the numerical value of the first verse in the Bible.

4. The numerical value of Israel is 541, being the 10th hexagonal star number.

5. The number ten coincides with the numerical value of the first letter of the Tetragrammaton and the name Israel.

8.7. CONCLUSION

The name *Israel* has been subject to extensive analysis. For millennia, rabbis and sages have been intrigued and investigated that divinely given name. Their investigation demonstrates a love of the Torah and their creative and ingenious capacity for insight. Rabbi *Israel* ben Eliezer, the Baal Shem Tov, taught that nothing happens by chance; even if a leaf blows in the wind, it does so because God wills it. Skeptics, on the other hand, especially in terms of *gematria*, will assert that a person can pick any numbers, find a pattern, and claim it is significant. Nevertheless, this writer believes it is worthwhile to explore these writings if the result is only with a grin, followed by a sigh when completed.

APPENDIX 1.

Table 17. Avot 5:24 Partially Adapted to Parallel Learnings

He used to say:	Parallel
At five years old a person should study the Scriptures.	Genesis 35: 9 *Then God appeared to Jacob again when he came from Paddan-aram, and He blessed him. 10 God said to him, "Your name is Jacob; You shall no longer be called Jacob, But Israel shall be your name." So He called him Israel.* (NASB)
at ten years for the Mishnah	Mishnah: Avot 1:1 All Israel have a share in the World to Come, as it is stated (Isaiah 60:21): '*And Your people are tzadikkim (righteous).' They shall inherit the land forever. They are the branch of My planting, the work of My hands, in which I take pride.* (Sanhedrin 90a) Mishnah: Avot 5:1 "By ten sayings the world was created."

at thirteen for the commandments	The *gematria* of the Hebrew word המצות = "*haMitzvot*," i.e., "The Commandments" is 541. [Numbers 36:13]. So too, is the *gematria* of Israel [ישראל].
	Harry Waton (1873–1959)
	The numerical value of these words יהוה אלהי ישראל Jehovah is the God of Israel, in the first aspect is 613.[1] This number is well known: it symbolizes the Torah and its commandments. The commandments are supposed to be 613 in number. But this is of no significance; of significance is this: the commandments are identified with Jehovah the God of Israel. [YHVH (26) +*Ehyeh* (46) + Israel (541) = 613]
at 15 for the Talmud	The Talmud Hullin 92a:
	The verse states: "*And he said: Your name shall no longer be called Jacob, but Israel; for you have striven with angels [elohim] and with men, and have prevailed.*"
at 18 for the bride chamber	Jeremiah 31:32. *not like the covenant which I made with their fathers on the day I took them by the hand to bring them out of the land of Egypt, My covenant which they broke, although I was a husband to them," declares the Lord.*
	Isaiah 54:5–6 *For your husband is your Maker, Whose name is the Lord of armies; And your Redeemer is the Holy One of Israel, Who is called the God of all the earth. For the Lord has called you, Like a wife forsaken and grieved in spirit, Even like a wife of one's youth when she is rejected," Says your God.* (NASB)
	Ľchah Dodi - Come, my Beloved, to meet the Bride; let us welcome the Shabbat.

1. According to tradition, there are 613 commandments: 248 positive and 365 negatives.

at 20 for one's life pursuit/righteousness/livelihood: Some Rabbis interpret this verse to mean that at twenty, he pursues the enemy in war. This is the age at which one is liable to join the army, according to the Torah (Number 1:3). Others believe he must pursue means to support his family or that by twenty a person should have a profession.	Rabbi Rachel Barenblat (the Velveteen Rabbi) (1975–) My teacher and friend Rabbi Arthur Waskow translates Israel as God-wrestler. Israel is the one who wrestles with God. And as we are the people Israel, the community which bears his name, then wrestling with God is our task, too. Perhaps this means wrestling with the texts in Torah which challenge us, or wrestling with ethical questions about what kind of life we intend to lead.
at 30 for authority/the peak of strength	The Talmud Hullin 92a: The verse states: "*And he said: Your name shall no longer be called Jacob, but Israel; for you have striven with angels [elohim] and with men, and have prevailed.*" Rabbi Meir Leibush Jehiel Michael Malbim (1809–1879) His blessing was that no more shall his name be called Yaqov but Yisrael, for he had triumphed with the power of his essential self and his inner soul. Hence, *for you have contended with angels and with men.* This is within you the godly power that derives from the soul, which is a godly portion from On-high, and the human power that derives from the physical-material – the voice of Yaqov and the hands of Esav –and with them have you won this battle

at 40 for discernment or understanding (Binah): At forty a person's wisdom comes to fruition. Traditionally this is the age at which a person can be considered a "rabbi." For example, the Talmud (*Avodah Zarah* 5b) records in the name of Rabbah that one does not truly understand his teacher until after forty years. Others suggest this is the age one can start the study of the kabbalah.	Rabbi Nathan Schapira (1606–1666) . . . The mystery of this is found in the passage in the *Zohar* talking about how "*Abba* is the Foundation of his daughter' (Pinchas 158a), which says that she is *Eretz Yisrael*, "*Yisrael Sabba*." She includes ten levels to correspond to the ten nations, those levels are *keter, hokhmah, binah, gedula (chesed), gevurah, tiferet, netzach, hod, yesod* and *malkhut*. The first letters of those ten levels equal "Yisrael" [541] [ישראל). There in the midst of *Eretz Yisrael*, ten levels of holiness sanctify it.[2]
at 50 for counsel: In order to give advice a person needs to be wise but he also needs experience.	The concept of *hokhmah*, that is "wisdom," is intimately connected with the first verse of the Torah (Genesis 1:1) and specifically the name Israel.
at 60 to be an elder/sagacity/old age	Genesis 25:26 *Afterward his brother came out with his hand holding on to Esau's heel, so he was named Jacob; and Isaac was sixty years old when she gave birth to them.*

2. Schapira, "Vanquishing the 'Lower 7.' Note: 20 +8 + 2 +3 + 3 + 400 + 50 + 5 + 10 + 40 = 541.

at 70 for gray hairs/fullness of years	David died at the age of seventy. He is described in the Hebrew Bible as second king of the United Kingdom of Israel (Israel and Judah). 1 Kings 2:1–4 *As David's time to die drew near, he commanded his son Solomon, saying, 2 "I am going the way of all the earth. So be strong, and prove yourself a man. 3 Do your duty to the Lord your God, to walk in His ways, to keep His statutes, His commandments, His ordinances, and His testimonies, according to what is written in the Law of Moses, so that you may succeed in all that you do and wherever you turn, 4 so that the Lord may fulfill His promise which He spoke regarding me, saying, 'If your sons are careful about their way, to walk before Me in truth with all their heart and all their soul, you shall not be deprived of a man to occupy the throne of Israel.' (NASB)*
at a 120	Deuteronomy 34:6, 10–11 *And He buried him in the valley in the land of Moab, opposite Beth-peor; but no one knows his burial place to this day . . .* *Since that time no prophet has risen in Israel like Moses, whom the Lord knew face to face, 11 for all the signs and wonders which the Lord sent him to perform in the land of Egypt against Pharaoh, all his servants, and all his land— (NSAB)*
and with your last breath.	*Hear O Israel, the Lord is our God, the Lord is One.*[3]

3. Birnbaum, *The Daily Prayer Book*, 26, 76; Kasher, *Sh'ma Yisrael*, 5–9; Lamm, *The Shema*, 1–57.

Appendix 2.

Table 18. The Appearance of the Name Israel in the Hebrew Bible [1]

Book of the Bible	*b'ne yiśîrāēl*	*yiśîrāēl* (all occurrences)
Genesis	7	43
Exodus	123	170
Leviticus	54	65
Numbers	171	237
Deuteronomy	21	72
Joshua	69	160
Judges	61	184
I Samuel	12	151
II Samuel	5	117
I Kings	21	203
II Kings	11	164
Isaiah	5	92
Jeremiah	9	125
Ezekiel	11	186
Hosea	6	44
Joel	1	3
Amos	5	30
Obadiah	1	1
Jonah	–	–

1. Gerlemann, "Israel," *Theological Lexicon of the Old Testament*, 2:582.

Micah	1	12
Nahum	–	1
Habakkuk	–	–
Zephaniah	–	4
Haggai	–	–
Zechariah	–	5
Malachi	–	5
Psalm	2	62
Job	–	–
Proverbs	–	1
Ruth	–	5
Song of Songs	–	1
Ecclesiastes	–	1
Lamentations	–	3
Esther	–	–
Daniel	1	4
Ezra	4	40
Nehemiah	9	40
1 Chronicles	4	22
2 Chronicles	23	187
OT [Hebrew Bible]	637	2514

APPENDIX 3.

The *El* Ending of Israel in Names

THE WORD *EL* (ALEPH *lamed*), 'God,' is common in proper names. At the beginning of a name, it usually appears as Eli (*aleph lamed yod*). The word is also found at the end of a name (e.g., Israel). A list of *El* ending names follows. *The Encyclopedia Biblica* provides an extensive entry.[1] Several categories of the *El* name adapted from that encyclopedia article include the following.

1. (= 27) God the giver

    a. God gives of his own free will, or apportions (as a gift)

    b. God increases (the family)

    c. God opens (the womb)

2. = 28 Gracious

    a. God *has mercy* [Jerahmeel]

    b. God *blesses* [Barachel]

    c. God *loves*

    d. God *helps* [Adriel, Azareel]

    e. God *is with man* [Immanuel, Ithiel]

    f. God *confers benefits* [Gamaliel, Mehetabeel]

    g. God *is good* [Tabeel]

---

1. Nöldeke, "Names," 3279–3285.

3. = 29 Strength

    a. God *holds fast* [Ezekiel]

    b. God is *strong, and strengthens* [Uzziel, Jaaziel]

    c. God is *a refuge* [Bazaleel]

4. = 30 Deliverer

    a. God *comforts*

    b. God *heals* [Raphael]

    c. God *redeems*

    d. God *preserves*

    e. God *keeps in safety?*

    f. God *conceals (i.e., presumably 'defends')*

5. = 31 Maker

    a. God *determines fate* [Gaddi-el]

    b. God *brings back* [Shuba-el, Shebu-el]

    c. God *places (?), sits on the throne* (?) [Jesime-el]

6. = 32 Knower

    a. God *sees* [Haza-el, Hazi-el, Jahaz-el]

    b. God *hears* [Ishmael]

7. = 34 Object

    a. God *is the object of praise* [Mahalal-el]

    b. God *is the object of a request* [Shealti-el]

8. = 38 Divine perfections

    a. *God is in front* [Kadmi-el]

    b. *God is incomparable* [Micha-el]

Appendix 4.

El Theophory

The following alphabetical list of names refer to *El* and their meanings in Hebrew[1]:

Abdiel– *Servant of God*

Abiel – *God my Father*

Abimael – *A Father sent from God*

Adbeel – *Disciplined of God*

Adiel – *Witness of God*

Adirael – *Magnificence of God*

Adriel – *Flock of God*

Advachiel – *Happiness of God*

Ambriel – *Energy of God*

Ammiel – *People of God*

Ariel – *Lion of God*

Armisael – *Mountain of Judgment of God*

Azael – *Whom God Strengthens*

Azazel – *God Strengthens* or *Arrogant to God*

Azrael – *Help of God*

Barakiel, Baraquiel – *Lightning of God*

1. Wikipedia, "Theophory in the Bible."

Barachiel, Bardiel – *Kindness of God* or *Ray of God*

Bethel – *House of God*

Betzalel – *Shadow/Path of God*

Bithiel – *Daughter of God*

Boel – *God is in Him*

Chakel – *Wisdom of God*

Chamuel – *He who Seeks God*

Cassiel – *Speed of God* or *God is my anger*

Denzel – Fortress of God

Daniel – *Judged by God* or *Judgement of God*

Elad – *God Forever*

Eliana – *My God Answers*

Elijah (Elias) – *Whose God is Jah, God Jah, The Strong [dubious] Jah, God of Jah, My God is Jah.* Reference to the meaning of both (Eli)–(Jah)

Elisha – *Salvation of God*

Elishama – *My God Hears*

Elishua – *God is my salvation*

Eliezer – *My God Helps*

Elimelech – *My God is King*

Elizabeth – *My God is Oath*

Elkanah – *God has Possessed*, or *God has Created*

Emmanuel – *God is with us*

Ezekiel – *God will Strengthen*

Ezequeel – *Strength of God*

Ezrael – *Help of God*

Gavriel – *Man of God, God has shown Himself Mighty, Hero of God* or *Strong one of God*

Gaghiel – *Roaring Beast of God*

Gamaliel – *Reward of God*

Hamaliel – *Grace of God*

Hanael – *Glory of God*

Harel – *"Mountain of God"*

Immanuel – *God with us*

Imriel – *Eloquence of God*

Iruel – *Fear of God*

Ishmael, Ishamael – *Heard by God, Named by God,* or *God Hearkens*

Israel, Yisrael – *Struggles with God* or *Prince of God*

Jekuthiel – *God will support*

Jerahmeel – *God's exaltation*

Jeremiel – *God's mercy*

Jezreel – *God will sow*

Joel - *Jah is God*

Jegudiel – *Glorifier of God*

Jophiel, Lophiel, Yofiel, Zophiel – *Beauty of God*

Katriel – *Crown of God*

Kazbiel – *He who lies to God*

Kushiel – *Rigid One of God*

Lee-El, Lee-el, Leeel – *For God*

Leliel – *Jaws of God*

Lemuel – *Dedicated to God*

Mahalalel – *The blessed God, The shining light of God,* or *The glory of God*

Malahidael – *King of God*

Matarael – *Premonition of God*

Michael – *Who is like God?* a question

Mishael – *Who is what God is?* a question

Nathanael, Nathaniel -- *Given by God* or *God has Given* or *"Gift of God"*

Nemuel – *Day of God*

Othiel – *Hour of God*

Peniel, Penuel, Phanuel – *Face of God*

Priel – *Fruit of God*

Rachmiel – *God is my Comforter*

Ramiel– *Thunder of God*

Raphael – *God is Healing* or *Healing one of God*

Raziel – *Secret of God*

Rameel – *Mercy of God* or *Compassion of God*

Reuel – *Friend of God*

Sachiel – *Price of God* or *Covering of God*

Salatheel – *I have asked God*

Sahaquiel – *Ingenuity of God*

Samael, Sammael – *Severity of God*, see also Samael (disambiguation)

Samiel – *Blind God*, epithet for Baal or the Demiurge

Samuel – *Name/Heard of God*

Sariel – *Command of God*

Sealtiel – *Intercessor of God*

Shamsiel – *Lonely Conqueror of God*

Shealtiel – *I asked God [for this child]*

Suriel – *Moon of God*

Tamiel – *Perfection of God*

Tarfiel – *God Nourishes*

Tzaphkiel – *Beholder of God*

Tzaphquiel – *Contemplation of God*

Uriel – *Sun of God, Light of God* or *Fire of God*

Uzziel – *Power from God*

Verchiel – *Shining of God*

Za'afiel– *Wrath of God*

Zadkiel – *Righteousness of God* (rabbinic)

Zagzagel – *Splendor of God*

Zaphkiel – *Knowledge of God*

Zeruel – *Arm of God*

Zophiel – *Beauty of God*

Zuriel – *Rock of God*

Appendix 5.

The Seventy Names Enumerated in the *Midrash Zuta* (*Midrash Shir HaShirim Zuta*)

Israel, Jeshurun, Firstborn, Youth, Gentle, Unique, Child, Brother, Friend, Beloved, Son, Slave, Nation (in Hebrew: Am), Nation (in Hebrew: Goy), Mother, Daughter, Spouse, Bride, A young wife, Jews, Hebrews, Lion, Leopard, Snake, Gazelle, Wolf, Ox, He-Goat, Vine, Plantation, Locked Garden, Orchard, Well spring, Friend, Redeemed, Sanctified, A Priestly Kingdom, Multitudes, Servants (of the Lord), Godly, Masters, Superior, United, Persons, Tribe, Convocation, Advocates of justice, Palm, Nut, Cluster of grapes, Fig, Pomegranate, Settlement, Amulet, Reed, Dove, Prickly, Sons of the living God, Pupil (of eye), Cow, Insect, Mother, Wise, Heroes, Righteous, Devout, Honest, Kinsman, Peoples, Innocent.[2]

2. Granot, "The Seventy Names of Israel." See Rabbi Gold's extensive notes on Jacob ben Asher, *Baal HaTurim Chumash: Bamidbar/Numbers,* 1486–489.

Appendix 6.

The Seventy-Three Occurrences of *Hevel* in the Hebrew Bible

Deuteronomy 32:21	Ecclesiastes 1:2	Ecclesiastes 7:15
1 Kings 16:13	Ecclesiastes 1:2	Ecclesiastes 8:10
1 Kings 16:26	Ecclesiastes 1:14	Ecclesiastes 8:14
2 Kgs 17:15	Ecclesiastes 2:1	Ecclesiastes 8:14
Job 7:16	Ecclesiastes 2:11	Ecclesiastes 9:9
Job 9:29	Ecclesiastes 2:15	Ecclesiastes 11:8
Job 21:34	Ecclesiastes 2:17	Ecclesiastes 11:10
Job 27:12	Ecclesiastes 2:19	Ecclesiastes 12:8
Job 35:16	Ecclesiastes 2:21	Ecclesiastes 12:8
Psalm 31:6	Ecclesiastes 2:23	Ecclesiastes 12:8
Psalm 39:5	Ecclesiastes 2:26	Isaiah 30:7
Psalm 39:6	Ecclesiastes 3:19	Isaiah 49:4
Psalm 39:11	Ecclesiastes 4:4	Isaiah 57:13
Psalm 62:9	Ecclesiastes 4:7	Jeremiah 2:5
Psalm 62:9	Ecclesiastes 4:8	Jeremiah 8:19
Psalm 78:33	Ecclesiastes 4:16	Jeremiah 10:3
Psalm 94:11	Ecclesiastes 5:7	Jeremiah 10:8
Psalm 144:4	Ecclesiastes 5:10	Jeremiah 10:15
Proverbs 13:11	Ecclesiastes 6:2	Jeremiah 14:22
Proverbs 21:6	Ecclesiastes 6:4	Jeremiah 16:19
Proverbs 31:30	Ecclesiastes 6:9	Jeremiah 51:18
Ecclesiastes 1:2	Ecclesiastes 6:11	Lamentation 4:17
Ecclesiastes 1:2	Ecclesiastes 6:12	Jonah 2:8
Ecclesiastes 1:2	Ecclesiastes 7:6	Zechariah 10:2

Bibliography

Abulafia, Abraham. Ms. Firenze-Laurenziana II:48, fols. 11b-12a

Albright, W. F. "The Names 'Israel' and 'Judah' with an Excursus on the Etymology of Todah and Torah." *Journal of Biblical Literature* 46, no. 3/4 (1927) 151–85. https://doi.org/10.2307/3260017.

Alt, Yehoshua. "The Fight For The 100 Brachos," http://www.nevehzion.org/wp-content/uploads/2018/11/Vayishlach-2018-Rabbi-Alt.pdf

Alter, Judah Aryeh Leib. *Sefat Emet: Rabbi Yehudah Leib Alter of Ger*. Translated by Akiva Roth.

Alter, Michael J. *What Is the Purpose of Creation?: A Jewish Anthology*. Northvale, NJ: Jason Aronson, 1991.

———. *Why the Torah Begins with the Letter Beit*. Northvale, NJ: Jason Aronson, 1998.

Alter, Robert. *Five Books of Moses—A Translation with Commentary*. New York: Norton, 2008.

Anonymous. Kitvei Qodesh. Translated by Larry Tabick. Jerusalem: A. Aminof, 1928.

Anonymous. (MS) No, 1822/MS Mich #460 [Part 123, f. 141–146]

Asher, Jacob ben. *Baal Haturim Chumash: The Torah with the Baal Haturim's Classic Commentary Translated, Annotated, and Elucidated: Numbers*. Translated by Eliyahu Touger. Brooklyn, NY: Mesorah, 2003.

———. *Perush Ba'al Ha-Ṭurim: 'al Ha-Torah = Baal HaTurim Chumash: The Torah with the Baal HaTurim's Classic Commentary*. Edited by Avie Gold, Eliyahu Touger, Nosson Scherman, and Meir Zlotowitz. Brooklyn, NY: Mesorah, 2004.

———. *Perush Ba'al Ha-Ṭurim: 'al Ha-Torah = Baal HaTurim Chumash*. Translated by Akiva Roth.

———. *Tur on the Torah: Commentary on the Torah*. Vol. 1. Translated by Eliyahu Munk. Jerusalem: Lambda, 2005.

Ashkenazi, Yaakov ben Yitzchak. *Tzeénah Ureénah:—"Go Ye and See." A Rabbinical Commentary on Genesis*. Translated by Paul Isaac Hershon. London: Hodder and Stoughton, 1885.

Azulai, Chaim Yosef David. "All Israel Has a Share in the World to Come." Pirkei Avot—with select commentaries—all Israel has a share in the world to come. https://www.dafyomi.co.il/general/info/ref/avot.php?d=2.

Bachya ben Asher, *Torah Commentary: Midrash Rabbeinu Bachya*. Translated and annotated Eliyahu Munk. Jerusalem: Urim, 2003.

Bar Tzadok, Ariel. "The Secret of David's Star & Solomon's Seal." In *The Evolution of God: Experiencing the Fractal Sefirot of the Kabbalah*, 341–71. Independently Published, 1993–2020.

Barenblat, Rachel. "Seeing the Wrestle as a Blessing: Thoughts on Vayishlach." Velveteen Rabbi. https://velveteenrabbi.blogs.com/blog/2013/11/seeing-the-wrestle-as-a-blessing-thoughts-on-vayishlach.html.

Bialik, Ḥayyim Naḥmān, and Yehoshua Hana Ravnitzky. *The Book of Legends = Sēfer Ha-Aggadah*. Translated by William G. Braude. New York: Schocken, 1992.

bible.ort.org. "Vayishlach." http://bible.ort.org/books/torahd5.asp?action=displaypage &book=1&chapter=33&verse=6&portion=8.

Birnbaum, Ellen. *The Place of Judaism in Philo's Thought: Israel, Jews, and Proselytes.* Atlanta: Scholars, 1996.

Birnbaum, Philip. *Daily Prayer Book.* New York: Hebrew Publishing, 1949.

Blech, Benjamin, and Elaine Blech. *Your Name Is Your Blessing: Hebrew Names and Their Mystical Meanings.* Lanham, MD: Jason Aronson, 2004.

Boerema, Joanne. "Sefer Ha-Ot: Between Individual and Historical Redemption." MA thesis, Universiteit Van Amsterdam, 2019. https://scripties.uba.uva.nl/download?fid=673390.

Bonder, Nilton. *Boundaries of Intelligence: Senses and Spirituality in Management.* Translated by Diane Grosklaus Whitty. Victoria, BC: Trafford, 2010.

Boruch, Dovid. *"Ma'amar Sod Etzba Elokim": A Deeper Look at the Makkos.* 3rd ed. LULU COM, 2019.

Burkeman, Danny. "Pride of Our Name,' World Union for Progressive Judaism." Torah from around the world #92 | World Union for Progressive Judaism. https://wupj.org/library/the-weekly-portion/934/torah-from-around-the-world-92/.

Chanoch ben Yaacov. "Parashat Bo Gematria." Gematria of parasha bo 5779, 2018. https://myemail.constantcontact.com/Gematria-of-Parasha-B5779.html?soid=11 02037575871&aid=plP44qt2Uxo.

———. "Shema Israel: Unity That Comes From Hearing." http://www.yeshshem.com/kabbalah-prayer-shemah.htm.

Cheyne, T. K. "Jacob." In *Encyclopaedia Biblica* 2:2306–311.

Claar, Fred. "Israel Means to Struggle with God." https://www.myjewishlearning.com/author/fred-claar/.

The Concise Oxford English Dictionary 10th ed. New York: Oxford University Press, 2002.

Coote, Robert. "The Meaning of the Name Israel." *Harvard Theological Review* 65, no. 1 (1972) 137–42. https://doi.org/10.1017/s0017816000002418.

Cordovero, Moses ben. *Moses Cordovero's Introduction to Kabbalah: An Annotated Translation of His or Ne'erav.* Translated by Ira Robinson. New York: Yeshiva University. Press, 1994.

Coughenour, Robert A. "A Conversation on Israel in the Bible." *Reformed Review* 33, no. 1 (1979) 16–30.

Culi, Jacob. *Meam Lo'ez.* Translated by Akiva Roth.

Danell, G.A. "Studies in the Name Israel in the Old Testament." Dissertation, Appelbergs Boktryckeri-aktiebolag, 1946.

David ben Abraham Maimuni. *Midrash Rabi David Ha-Nagid.* Edited by Abraham I. Katsh. Translated by Ephraim Simon. Jerusalem: Mosad ha-Rav Kook, 1964.

Delcau, Stacey Frishman. "The Story of the Magen David." https://docslib.org/doc/9834882/the-story-of-the-magen-david.

Diop, Ganoune. "The Name Israel and Related Expressions in the Books of Amos and Hosea." PhD diss., Andrews University, 1995. http://digitalcommons.andrews.edu/dissertations/35

Dubov, Nissan David. *Discovering Jewish Mysticism*. New York: Dwelling Place, 2006.

———. *"The Key to Kabbalah: Discovering Jewish Mysticism*. New York: Dwelling Place, 2006.

Duncan, William F. "Genesis 111." Star Triangle Code. https://www.startriangle2012.com/genesis-111.

Eisenberg, Ronald L. *The JPS Guide to Jewish Traditions*. Philadelphia: Jewish Publication Society, 2004.

Eleazar ben Judah, of Worms. *Sefer ha-Shem* (MS British Museum 737, fol. 203a.

———. *Sefer ha-Hokhmah* MS Oxford 1812, fols. 101b–102a (cf. also MS JTS 1786 fol. 43a.

———. "Sefer Ha-Shem." In *Through a Speculum That Shines: Vision and Imagination in Medieval Jewish Mysticism*. Translated by Elliot R. Wolfson, 254. Princeton: Princeton University Press, 1994.

———. *Perushe sidur ha-tefilah la-Roḳeaḥ*. Edited by Moshe Hesler. Jerusalem, Mekhon ha-Rav Hershler, 1992.

Emden, Jacob. *Sidur Ha-Yaʿavets: Bet Yaʿaḳov = The Siddur Yaʾavetz*. Translated by Akiva Roth.

Ephraim Solomon ben Aaron Luntshits. "'For You Have Striven with God and with Men'—Yaakov's Dual Destiny in Kli Yakar." https://torah.etzion.org.il/en/you-have-striven-god-and-men-%E2%80%93-yaakovs-dual-destiny.

Epstein, Baruch ha-Levi. *Torah Temimah*. Translated by Akiva Roth.

Epstein, Isidore, ed. *Niddah: Translated into English with Notes, Glossary and Indices*. Translated by Israel W. Slotki. London: Soncino, 1948.

Even-Shoshan, Abraham, ed. *A New Concordance of the Bible: Thesaurus of the Language of the Bible: Hebrew and Aramaic: Roots, Words, Proper Names, Phrases and Synonyms*. Jerusalem: Kiryat Sefer, 2015.

Evron, Oren. "Code of Creation Part 1—The Discovery in Genesis 1:1 (בראשית ברא אלהים את השמים ואת הארץ)." https://www.youtube.com/watch?v=ikGLJHNcJLo&t=281s.

———. "Genesis and Pi." Pi and Genesis. https://www.dafyomi.co.il/general/info/torahau/torah_numerology.php?d=5.

Finkel, Avraham Yaakov. *In My Flesh I See God: A Treasury of Rabbinic Insights about the Human Anatomy*. Northvale, NJ: Aronson, 1995.

Fischlewitz, Boruch. "Vayishlach." https://www.613montreal.com/blog/blogger/boruch44.

Fox, Everett. *The Five Books of* Moses. New York: Schocken, 1995.

Gelman, Lilly. "The Star of David: Between Judaism and Zionism." *Moment Magazine*. https://momentmag.com/the-star-of-david-between-judaism-and-zionism/

Gerleman, G. "Israel." In *Theological Lexicon of the Old Testament*, edited by Ernst Jenni and with the assistance of Claus Westermann, translated by Mark E. Biddle, 581–584. Peabody, MA: Hendrickson, 1997.

Ginsburgh, Yitzchak. "The Angel Michaʾel." GalEinai—Revealing the Torah's Inner Dimension. https://www.inner.org/parshah/genesis/vayeira/E68–0211.php.

———. *The Hebrew Letters: Channels of Creative Consciousness*. Jerusalem: Gal Einai, 1990.

———. *Living in Divine Space: Kabbalah and Meditation*. Jerusalem: Linda Pinsky, 2003.

Ginzberg, Louis. *The Legends of the Jews*, Vol 5. Philadelphia: Jewish Publication Society, 1925.

Glazerson, Matityahu. *Building Blocks of the Soul: Studies on the Letters and Words of the Hebrew Language*. Northvale, NJ: Jason Aronson, 1997.

———. *Letters of Fire: Mystical Insights into the Hebrew Language*. New York: Feldheim, 1991.

———. *Torah, Light and Healing: Mystical Insights into Healing Based on the Hebrew Language*. Northvale, NJ: Jason Aronson, 1996.

Granot, Archie. "Limited Edition Lasercuts." https://archiegranotcatalog.com/online-store/limited-edition-lasercuts.

Green, Arthur. "Introduction." In *The Zohar: Pritzker Edition* 1, edited by Daniel C. Matt, xxi-liii. Stanford: Stanford University Press, 2004.

Guggenheimer, Heinrich W., trans. "Jerusalem Talmud Taanit 2:6." Sefaria, https://www.sefaria.org/Jerusalem_Talmud_Taanit.2.6?lang=bi&with=all&lang2=en.

Hadassi, Judah ben Elijah. *Eshkol Ha-Kofer*. Gozlva, 1836. https://www.hebrewbooks.org/44048.

Haralick, Robert M. *The Inner Meaning of the Hebrew Letters*. Lanham, MD: Rowman & Littlefield, 2005.

Harvey, Graham Alan Peter. "The True Israel: Uses of the Names Jew, Hebrew and Israel in Ancient Jewish Literature." PhD Diss., University of Newcastle upon Tyne, 1991.

Hasan-Rokem, Galit. "The Star of David and the Stars Outside: The Poetics and Semiotics of Jewish Folklore and of Zionism." *Images* 9, no. 1 (2016) 78–89. https://doi.org/10.1163/18718000–12340066.

Hayward, C. T. "Philo, the Septuagint of Genesis 32:24–32 and the Name 'Israel': Fighting the Passions, Inspiration and the Vision of God." *Journal of Jewish Studies* 51, no. 2 (2000) 209–26. https://doi.org/10.18647/2274/jjs-2000.

Hayward, Robert. *Interpretations of the Name Israel in Ancient Judaism and Some Early Christian Writings: from Victorious Athlete to Heavenly Champion*. Oxford: Oxford University Press, 2005.

Hezekiah ben Manoah. *Chizkuni: Torah Commentary*. Translated by Eliyahu Munk. Brooklyn, NY: Ktav, 2013.

Hirsch, Samson Raphael, and Isaac Levy. *The Pentateuch: Genesis*. Vol. 1. Gateshead: Judaica, 1989.

Hlava, Baḥya ben Asher ben. *Midrash Rabbeinu Bachya: Torah Commentary*. Translated by Eliyahu Munk. Brooklyn, NY: Ktav, 1998.

Horowitz, Isaiah. *The Generation of Adam*. Translated by Miles Krassen. New York: Paulist, 1996.

———. *Shney Luchot Habrit*. Translated by Eliyahu Munk. Jerusalem: Munk, 1992.

Ibn-'Ezra, Avraham Ben-Me'ir. *Ibn Ezra's Commentary on the Pentateuch*. Translated by Akiva Roth.

Idel, Moshe. *Abraham Abulafia's Esotericism: Secrets and Doubts*. Edited by Racheli Haliva. Berlin: De Gruyter, 2020.

———. *Absorbing Perfections: Kabbalah and Interpretation*. New Haven: Yale University Press, 2002.

———. *Language, Torah, and Hermeneutics in Abraham Abulafia*. Translated by Menahem Kallus. Albany, NY: State University of New York Press, 1989.

———. "On Paradise in Jewish Mysticism." *Journal for the Study of Religions and Ideologies* 10, no. 30 (2010) 1–38.

Israel, Alex. "Vayishlach Jacob, Esau and the Angel: The Transformation of Yaakov." https://www.alexisrael.org/vayishlach-jacob-struggles.

Israel Ministry of Foreign Affairs. "King Solomon's Seal." https://mfa.gov.il/mfa/mfa-archive/1999/pages/king%20solomon-s%20seal.aspx.

Jack, J.W. "The Israel Stele of Merenptah." *The Expository Times* 36, no. 1 (1924) 40–44. https://doi.org/10.1177/001452462403600108.

Jacobs, Joseph. "Names (Personal)," In *The Jewish Encyclopedia* 9:152–60.

Jehiel, Asher ben. *Sefer Hadar Zeḳenim: 'al Ḥameshet Ḥumshe Ha-Torah.* Translated by Ephraim Simon. Jerusalem: Bene-Berak, 1986.

Jenkins, Vernon. *The Second Edge: A Role for Numerical Coincidence in the Pursuit of Truth.* Mentor. http://www.whatabeginning.com/book.pdf

Josephus, Flavius. *The Complete Works of Josephus.* Translated by William Whiston. Grand Rapids: Kregel, 1960.

Kaplan, Aryeh. *The Bahir: An Ancient Kabbalistic Text Attributed to Rabbi Nehuniah Ben Hakana, First Century, C.E.* New York: Samuel Weiser, 1979.

———. *Sefer Yetzirah = the Book of Creation: In Theory and Practice.* York Beach, ME: S. Weiser, 1990.

Kasher, Menachem M. *Encyclopedia of Biblical Interpretation (Torah Shelemah).* Translated by Harry Freeman. American Biblical Encyclopedia Society, 1953.

———. *Sh'ma Yisra'él: The Jewish Affirmation of Faith: Reflections on Its Levels of Meaning.* Jerusalem: Torah Shelemah Institute, 1974.

Kimchi, David. *Torah Commentary Mikraot Gedolot: Multi-commentary on the Torah,* Vol. 2. Translated and annotated Eliyahu Munk. Jerusalem: Lambda, 2006.

Ki-Tov, Elijah. *Sefer ha-Parahot.* Translated by Ephraim Simon. Jerusalem: "ALEF" Machon Lehozaat Sefarim, 1961.

Kogan, Leonid Efimovich. "The Etymology of Israel (with an Appendix on Non-Hebrew Semitic Names among Hebrews in the Old Testament." In *Babel Und Bibel,* edited by Natalia V. Koslova, S. V. Lëzov, Serguei Tishchenko, and Leonid Efimovich Kogan, 237–55. Winona Lake, IN: Published for the Russian State University for the Humanities by Eisenbrauns, 2006.

Koren Talmud Bavli, Vol 37: Hullin Part 1, English Edition. Jerusalem: Koren, 2015.

Kornfeld, Mordecai. "The Number of Letters in the Torah." https://www.dafyomi.co.il/kidushin/insites/kd-dt-030.htm

Lamm, Norman. *The Shema: Spirituality and Law in Judaism as Exemplified in the Shema the Most Important Passage in the Torah.* Philadelphia: Jewish Publication Society, 1998.

Lancaster, Brian L. "On the Relationship Between Cognitive Models and Spiritual Maps Evidence from Hebrew Language Mysticism." *Journal of Consciousness Studies* 7, no. 11–12 (2000) 231–50.

Leibtag, Menachem. "Vayishlach: From Yaakov to Yisrael—Part 2—Rabbi Menachem Leibtag on Parsha." https://outorah.org/p/37215/.

Levi Yitzchok of Bereditchev. *Kedushat Levi: Torah Commentary.* Translated by Eliyahu Munk. Vol. 1. Brooklyn, NY: Lambda, 2009.

Lifshitz, Joseph Isaac. *Rabbi Meir of Rothenburg and the Foundation of Jewish Political Thought.* New York: Cambridge University Press, 2016.

Locks, Gutman. "Gematria," Mystical Paths, https://www.mpaths.com/2009/04/gematria.html#!

———. *The Spice of Torah-Gematria*. New York: Judaica, 1985.

Maimonides, Moses ben. *The Guide for the Perplexed*. Translated by M. Friedländer. 2nd ed. New York: Dover, 1956.

Malbim, Meir Leibush ben Yechiel Michel. *Malbim Commentary on the Torah*. Translated by Zvi Faier. Vol. 3. M.P., 1982.

Marcus, Ralph. "The Hebrew Sibilant Sin and the Name Yisraʼel." *Journal of Biblical Literature* 60, no. 2 (1941) 141–50. https://doi.org/10.2307/3262361.

Matt, Daniel C., ed. *Zohar: Pritzker Edition*. Vol. 1. Stanford: Stanford University Press, 2004.

Meiliken, Jeffrey. "The Ultimate Reality Behind the Universe—Kabbalah Secrets." https://kabbalahsecrets.com/the-ultimate-reality-behind-the-universe/.

Melamed, Zalman Baruch. "For the Sake of the Beginning: Rabbi Zalman Baruch Melamed: Beit Midrash." https://www.yeshiva.co/midrash/964.

Midrash Rabbah: Genesis. 3rd ed. Vol. 2. Translated by Harry Freedman. London: Soncino, 1983.

Midrash Tanhuma / (S. Buber Recension). Vol. 2, *Exodus and Leviticus*. Translated by John T. Townsend. Hoboken, NJ: Ktav, 1989.

Mishory, Alec. "The Flag and the Emblem." https://embassies.gov.il/MFA/AboutIsrael/Israelat50/Pages/The%20Flag%20and%20the%20Emblem.aspx

Morgenstern, Julian. *A Jewish Interpretation of The Book of Genesis*. Cincinnati: The Union of American Hebrew Congregations, 1919.

Moses ben Nahman (Nachmanides). *Commentary on the Torah. Genesis*. Translated by Charles Ber Chavel. New York: Shilo, 1971.

Moshe Hayyim Ephraim of Sudilkov. "Degel Machaneh Ephraim, VeEthChanan (68d)." Translated by Akiva Roth.

Moshe Hayyim Ephraim of Sudilkov, and Shaul Magid. *Degel Mahane*. See "Divination and 'Incarnational Thinking' in Hasidism: An Overview." In *Hasidism Incarnate Hasidism, Christianity, and the Construction of Modern Judaism*, 15–30. Stanford: Stanford University Press, 2015. https://doi.org/10.1515/9780804793469-004

Munk, Eliyahu. *The Just Lives by His Faith: Essays on Topics Which Challenge Our Faith in Torah and Its Exponents*. Jerusalem, Israel: Munk, 1996.

Munk, Michael L. *The Wisdom in the Hebrew Alphabet*. New York: Mesorah, 1983.

Neusner, Jacob. *The Incarnation of God: The Character of Divinity in Formative Judaism*. Atlanta: Scholars, 1992.

New World Encyclopedia contributors. "Star of David." https://www.newworldencyclopedia.org/p/index.php?title=Star_of_David&oldid=1030164.

Nöldeke, Theodor. "Names." In *Encyclopedia Biblica*, 3:3271–331.

Norman, Robert A. *The Star of David: A Popular History of the Mysterious Hexagram*. New York: Kodesh, 2016.

Oegema, Gerbern S. *The History of the Shield of David: The Birth of a Symbol*. Frankfurt am Main: P. Lang, 1996.

Origen. "Commentary on the Gospel of John (Book II)." Translated by Allan Menzies. Church Father: Commentary on John, Book II (Origen). http://www.newadvent.org/fathers/101502.htm.

Ostropoli, Samson ben of. *Shemesh u-Magen*. Jerusalem, 1891. https://www.hebrewbooks.org/7308

The Oxford English Dictionary. Edited by John A. Simpson. Oxford: Clarendon, 1991.

The Oxford English Dictionary 2nd ed. Volume 10. Oxford: Oxford University Press, 1989.

Paluch, Agata. "The Enoch-Metatron Tradition in the Kabbalah of Nathan Neta Shapira of Krakow (1585–1633), PhD Diss." University College London, 2013. https://discovery.ucl.ac.uk/id/eprint/1404057/.

Park, Hana. "In the Beginning: A Book Arts Exploration of the Creation Account in Genesis." MA thesis, Massey University, Auckland, New Zealand, 2009. https://mro.massey.ac.nz/bitstream/handle/10179/1280/02whole.pdf

Philo (of Alexandria). *The Works of Philo Judæus, the Contemporary of Josephus.* Translated by Charles Duke Yonge. London: G. Bell & Sons, 1894.

———. *Philo.* Translated by Francis Henry Colson and G. H. Whitaker. Vol. 5. Cambridge, Mass: Harvard University Press, 1934.

———. *Philo, Supplement 1: Questions and Answers on Genesis.* Translated by Ralph Marcus. Cambridge, MA: Harvard University Press, 1932.

Plaut, W. Gunther. *The Magen David: How the Six-Pointed Star Became an Emblem for the Jewish People.* Washington, D.C.: B'nai B'rith Books, 1991.

———. *The Torah: A Modern Commentary.* New York: Union of American Hebrew Congregations, 1981.

Rashi. "Rashi on Genesis 32:29:1." Translated by M. Rosenbaum and A. M. Silberman. Sefaria. https://www.sefaria.org/Rashi_on_Genesis.32.29.1?lang=bi&with=all&lang2=en.

Raskin, Aaron L. "Chirik — Frozen Giver—Essentials—Chabad," https://www.chabad.org/library/article_cdo/aid/137301/jewish/Chirik-Frozen-Giver.htm.

———. *Letters of Light.* Brooklyn, NY: Sichos in English, 2003.

Recanati, Menachem. "Recanati on the Torah, Vayishlach 18." Sefaria, https://www.sefaria.org/Recanati_on_the_Torah%2C_Vayishlach.18?lang=bi&with=all&lang2=en.

Reifmann, Jacob. "Magen David." Translated by Ze'ev Barkan. http://star-of-david.blogspot.com/2014/12/magen-david-article-by-jacob-reifmann.html.

Rosenberg, Judah Yudel. *Sefer Peri Yehuda.* Translated by Ephraim Simon. sn.: Bilgora, 1935.

Saba, Avrahem. *Tzror Hamor: Torah Commentary*, Vol. 2. Translated by Eliyahu Munk. Jerusalem: Lambda, 2008.

Sachsse, Eduard. "Die Etymologie Und Älteste Aussprache Des Namens לארשי." *Zeitschrift für die Alttestamentliche Wissenschaft* 34, no. 1 (1914) 1–15. https://doi.org/10.1515/zatw.1914.34.1.1.

Sacks, Jonathan. "I Believe: A Weekly Reading of the Jewish Bible," on parshat Vayishlach, Koren Publishers, September 2022.

Samuel ben Meir (Rashbam), *Mikraot Gedolot: Multi-commentary on the Torah,* Vol. 2. Translated and annotated Eliyahu Munk. Jerusalem: Lambda, 2006.

Sarna, Nahum M. *The JPS Torah Commentary: Genesis.* Philadelphia: Jewish Publication Society, 1989.

Schapira, Natan. *Tuv Ha'aretz,* "Vanquishing the 'Lower 7'—Chapter Two, Part 2—Tuv Ha'aretz." Translated by David Slavin. www.yeshshem.com

Scherman, Nosson. *Kaddish: The Kaddish Prayer.* Brooklyn, NY: Mesorah, 1980.

Schochet, J. Immanuel . *Mystical Concepts in Chassidism.* Brooklyn, NY: Kehot, 1988.

Scholem, Gershom. "Gematria." In *Encyclopedia Judaica,* 7:426.

———. *Hatakh Ha-Zahav, Hotam Shelomohu-Magen-David.* Poalim, 1990.

———. *Major Trends in Jewish Mysticism.* New York: Schocken, 1961.

———. *On the Kabbalah and Its Symbolism.* Translated by Ralph Manheim. New York: Schocken Books, 1965.

———. "The Star of David: History of a Symbol." In *The Messianic Idea in Judaism and Other Essays on Jewish Spirituality.* Translated by Michael Meyer, 257–81. New York: Schocken, 1971.

Scholem, Gershom, and Melila Hellner-Eshed. "The Zohar." In *Encyclopedia Judaica*, 21:647–64.

Schwartz, Howard. *Tree of Souls: The Mythology of Judaism.* Oxford: Oxford University Press, 2004.

Sebag, Yosef. "Genesis and Pi." Pi and Genesis. https://www.dafyomi.co.il/general/info/torahau/torah_numerology.php?d=5.

———. "Star of David." Central prime. https://www.dafyomi.co.il/general/info/torahau/torah_numerology.php?d=16.

———. *Torah Numerology: Hidden Mathematical Codes in Genesis 1:1.* Author, 2020.

Shanks, Herschel. "When did ancient Israel begin?" *Biblical Archaeology Review* 38 (2012) 59–67.

Sheinkin, David. *Path of the Kabbalah.* New York: Paragon House, 1999.

Shimon bar Yochai. "The Source of All Blessing—When Worthy, Israel Draws the Dew of Blessing to the World Based on *Metok MiDevas.*" Translated by Samuel-Simcha Triester. https://www.chabad.org/kabbalah/article_cdo/aid/379533/jewish/The-Source-of-All-Blessing.htm.

Shimshon of Ostropoli. *Shemesh U'Magen*, 1891. https://www.hebrewbooks.org/7308.

Shneur Zalman of Lyady (Liadi) *Likutei Amarim Tanya.* Translated by Kehot. Brooklyn, NY: Kehot, 1984.

Silberberg, Naftali. "Star of David: The Mystical Significance—Kabbalistic . . .—Chabad." https://www.chabad.org/library/article_cdo/aid/788679/jewish/Star-of-David-The-Mystical-Significance.htm.

Sofer, Moses. *Commentary on the Torah.* Translated by Akiva Roth. Bratislava, 1879.

Stamm, Johann Jakob. "Names," *Encyclopedia Judaica* 14:764–66.

Stern, Samuel M. "'The First in Thought Is the Last in Action': The History of a Saying Attributed to Aristotle." *Journal of Semitic Studies* 7, no. 2 (1962) 234–52. https://doi.org/10.1093/jss/7.2.234.

Strong, James. *The Exhaustive Concordance of the Bible: Showing Every Word of the Text of the Common English Version of the Canonical Books, and Every Occurrence of Each Word in Regular Order; Together with a Comparative Concordance of the Authorized and Revised Versions, Including the American Variations; Also Brief Dictionaries of the Hebrew and Greek Words of the Original, with References to the English Words.* New York: Eaton & Mains, 1890.

———. "Hevel." Strong's Hebrew: 1892. הֶבֶל (Hebel) — 73 occurrences. https://biblehub.com/hebrew/strongs_1892.htm.

Tanna D'Vei Eliyahu. *Tanna Děbe Eliyyahu: The Lore of the School of Elijah.* Translated by William Gordon Braude and Israel James Kapstein. Philadelphia: Jewish Publication Society of America, 1981.

"Theophory in the Bible." Wikipedia. Wikimedia Foundation. https://en.wikipedia.org/wiki/Theophory_in_the_Bible.

Tishby, Isaiah, ed. *The Wisdom of the Zohar: An Anthology of Texts.* Translated by David Goldstein. Vol. 3. Oxford: The Littman Library of Jewish Civilization, 1987.

Trachtenberg, Joshua. *Jewish Magic Superstition: A Study in Folk Religion.* New York: Behrman's Jewish Book House, 1939.

Trugman, Avraham Arieh. *Secrets of the Magen David.* Mevo Modi'im: Ohr Chadash, 2013.

———. *Walking in the Fire: Classical Torah/Kabbalistic Meditations, Practices & Prayers.* Tarzana, CA: KosherTorah, 2007.

Ulmer, Rivka. "The Jerusalem Temple in Pesiqta Rabbati: From Creation to Apocalypse," *Hebrew Studies* 51 (2010) 223–59.

Waton, Harry. *The Key to the Bible.* New York: Spinoza Institute of America, 1952.

Wisnefsky, Moshe Yaakov. *Apples from the Orchard: Mystical Insights on the Weekly Torah Portion from Rabbi Yitzchak Luria—The Arizal.* Malibu, CA: Chabad of Malibu Thirty-Seven Books, 2008.

Wolfson, Elliot R. *Language, Eros, Being: Kabbalistic Hermeneutics and Poetic Imagination.* New York: Fordham University Press, 2005.

———. *Mekhilta De-Rabbi Shimon Bar Yohai.* Translated by Akiva Roth.

Yoreh, Tzemah. "Jacob Is Renamed Israel (Twice): Why Does His Name Remain Jacob?" https://www.thetorah.com/article/jacob-is-renamed-israel-twice-why-does-the-name-jacob-remain.

Zakovitch, Yair. *Jacob: Unexpected Patriarch.* Translated by Valerie Zakovitch. Yale University Press, 2012.

Zobel, H.-J. "Yisira'el." In *Theological Dictionary of the Old Testament* 6:397–420.

The Zohar: Yitro—Mishpatim. Vol. 10. Translated by Michael Berg. New York: Kabbalah Centre International, 2003.

Zwickel, Wolfgang and Pieter van der Veen, "The earliest reference to Israel and its possible archaeological and historical background," *Vetus Testamentum* 67 (2017) 129–40.

Names Index

BIBLICAL PERSONALITIES

Abram (Avram) or Abraham
(Avraham), vi, xiv–xv, 3–4,
23–24, 26, 30–31, 37, 45–46,
49–50, 63, 69, 81, 97
Adam, 18, 22, 46, 48–49, 74–75, 97,
104, 124

Betzalel (or Bezalel), xiii, 137, 139

David, 31, 47, 57, 109–110, 112, 114,
133

Elijah, 47
Esau (Esav), 21, 27–28, 31–32, 34–36,
42, 65, 74–75, 76n1, 81–82,
84–85, 88, 131–32
Esther, 61n44
Eve, 48

Goliath, 47

Haman, 61n44
Hannah, 50

Isaac (Yitzchak), 3–4, 21, 23, 26, 30,
30n15, 45, 49–50, 67, 76, 81,
97, 100, 110, 119–20, 132
Israel, x, xii, xv, xix, 1, 3, 5, 6n7, 8, 11–
12, 19, 21–30, 30n15, 32–39,
42, 44–45, 66–67, 73–76, 76n1,
78, 80–81, 84–85, 91, 97, 100,
119–20

Israel ben Eliezer (the Baal Shem Tov),
102, 127

Jacob (Yaakov, Ya'akov, Yakov), ix, xii,
xiv–xv, 1, 3–4, 7n10, 8, 11–12,
21–38, 42, 44–45, 47, 49–50,
57–58, 65–67, 69, 71–77,
80–84, 86, 88–92, 92n7, 95, 97,
100, 119–20, 125–26, 129–31
Jeremiah, 33, 56
Jeshurun (Yeshurun), 11
Jethro, 24
Joseph, 49, 49n18
Joshua, 4, 24
Judah (Yehudah), 11, 71n2

Leah, 45, 49–50, 64, 119
Lavan, 74, 82, 88

Mordecai, 61n44
Moses, 18, 47, 49, 52, 56, 65n56

Noah, 46, 49, 56

Rachel, 45, 49–50, 119
Rebekah (Rebecca), 45, 50, 58, 67,
119–20

Sarah (Sari), 24, 45, 49–50, 64–65, 81,
119
Saul, 47
Shem, 48
Solomon, 47

RABBINIC PERSONALITIES

Ahavah son of R. Ze'ra, 70
Akiva, 71

Berekhiah, 71

Eliezer b. Yose ha-Gelili, 52, 55

Ham b. Hanina, 28
Huna, 85n32

Judah, xiii

Kahana, 5

Phinehas, 71
Reuben, 71

Samuel b. R. Isaac, 70, 85n32
Simeon ben Laqish, 70

Yannai, 70
Yehudah, 61
Yohai, Simeon ben, 10, 28, 91n5,
        98n20

Zechariah, 8

NAMES

Abraham ben David Maimuni
        [Abraham, David ben (David
        ben Abraham Maimuni)], 73n9
Abulafia, Abraham, xvi, 58–59, 60n42,
        88
Albright, W.F., 6
Alt, Yehoshua, 67
Alter, Judah Aryeh [of Ger], 76
Alter, Michael J., x, 18n26, 51n25
Alter, Robert, xv, 37
Amenhotep III, 5
Arizal (Isaac ben Solomon Luria), 42,
        110n13, 111, 121
Antokolski, Mark, 114
Asher ben Jehiel, 54

Ashkenazi, Jacob ben Isaac (Yaakov
        ben Yitzchak), 33
Azulai, Chaim David Joseph (Hayyim
        Yoseph David Azulai) ("Hida"),
        10, 64

Bachya ben Asher, 8–9, 31, 88
Barkan, Ze'ev, 114
Barenblat, Rachel, 38, 131
Barras, Jeremy, x
Bar Tzadok, Ariel, xii–xiii, 109n9
Berg, Michael, 92n6–7
Bialik, Hayyim Nahman, 71n4
bible.ort.org., 39
Birnbaum, Ellen, 26n3, 27n4
Birnbaum, Philip, 133n3
Blech, Benjamin, xiv
Blech, Elaine, xiv
Boerema, Joanne, 59
Bonder, Nilton, 66
Boruch, Dovid, 62n46, 48
Burkeman, Danny, 83

Chanoch ben Yaacov, 62n50
Cheyne, T.K., 6n9, 7n10
Claar, Fred, 80
The Concise Oxford English Dictionary,
        xi
Coote, Robert, 6
Cordovero, Moses ben, 11, 12n22,
Coughenour, Robert A., 7
Culi, Yaakov, 73

Danell, G.A., 7, 43
David ben Abraham Maimuni, 73n9
Delcau, Stacey Frishman, 109n11
Diop, Ganoune, 6n9
Dubov, Nissan Dovid, 98
Duncan, William F., 102n1

Eisenberg, Ronald L., xiii
Eleazar ben Judah of Worms, xvi, 17,
        44, 49n17, 53, 57, 72
Emden, Jacob (Ya'avetz), xvii, 63,
        99n25
Ephraim Solomon ben Aaron of
        Luntshit, 73
Epstein, Baruch ha-Levi, 77

Even-Shoshan, Abraham, 3
Evron, Oren, 102n1, 105n2, 3, 106n5,
    6, 7

Fine, Steven, 113
Finkel, Avraham Yaakov, 94
Fischlewitz, Boroch, 84
Fox, Everett, 38

Gavriel (angel), 65, 88–89
Gerleman, G., 7n10
Gikatilla, Joseph ben Abraham, 9
Ginsburgh, Yitzchak, xvi, 19, 40n1,
    41n2, 43n8–9, 52n26, 64–65,
    66n58, 101
Ginzberg, Louis, 7
Glazerson, Matitiyahu, xvi, 12n24, 55,
    65, 65n56, 80,
Görg, Manfred, 5–6
Green, Arthur, 96

Haralick, Robert M., 12n24, 43n8–9
Harvey, Graham A.P., 5n4
Hezekiah ben Manoah, 31
Hirsch, Samson Raphael, 35
Horowitz, Isaiah, 44, 60, 92
Horowitz, Pinchas, 76

Ibn Ezra, Abraham, 72, 85n32
Idel, Moshe, 10, 59, 59n40, 60, 87, 113
Israel, Alex, 82
Israel Ministry of Foreign Affairs,
    109n9

Jack, J.W., 5n5
Jacob ben Asher, 32, 142n2
Jenkins, Vernon, 102n1
Josephus, 27, 39

Kaplan, Aryeh, xiiin6, xvii, 46n13, 79,
    95–96, 96n15, 16, 18
Kasher, Menachem M., 35, 71n5,
    133n3
Kimchi, David ("RaDak"), 30
Ki-Tov, Elijah, 55n34
Kogan, Leonid, 6n7
Kornfeld, Mordecai, 46n12

Lancaster, Brian L., 88, 88n3
Leibtag, Menachem, 38
Lifshitz, Joseph Isaac, 58n2
Locks, Gutman, 12n24, 13
Luzzato, Moses Hayyim ("Ramhal"),
    117

Maimonides, Moses ben Maimon
    ("Rambam"), 9
Malbim, Meir Leibush Jehiel Michael,
    34, 131
Marcus, Ralph, 6n7
Matt, Daniel C., 91n5
Meiliken, Jeffrey, 82, 98, 98n22
Melamed, Zalman Baruch, 85, 86n33
Merneptah, 5, 36
Midrash Tanhuma, 4
Mishory, Alec, 115
Morgenstern, Julian, 78
Moses ben Nahman (Nachmanides),
    the Ramban, xiv, 30
Moses de Leon (Moses ben Shem Tov
    de Leon), 9, 91–92
Moshe Hayyim Ephraim of Sudilkov,
    74
Munk, Eliyahu, xxi, 36, 60
Munk, Michael L., 11, 12n24, 40n1, 41,
    43n8–9, 51n24

Nachmanides, Moses ben Nahman,
    30, 32
Neusner, Jacob, 99n28
New World Encyclopedia contributors,
    111
Nöldeke, Theodore, 136n1
Norman, Robert A. 109n9
Nussenblatt, Naftali, 114, 114n22

Oegema, Gerbern S., 111, 112n17
Origen, 23
The Oxford English Dictionary, xi

Paluch, Agata, 44n10
Philo Judaeus (Philo of Alexandria),
    25–27
Plaut, Gunter, 36, 109n9

Raphael (Repha'el) (angel), 65, 137, 141

Rashi (Shlomo/Solomon ben Isaac), xv,
     10, 24n3, 29, 31, 44, 80
Raskin, Aaron L., xvi, 12, 40n1, 41–42,
     43n8–9, 51n24, 82n26
Recanati, Menachem ben Binyamin,
     11, 30, 79n21
Reifmann, Jacob, 109n9
Rosenberg, Judah Yudel, 77

Saba, Abraham ben Jacob, 73
Sachsse, Eduard, 6
Sacks, Jonathan, xvi, 81
Samuel ben Meir ("Rashbam"), 29
Sarna, Nahum M., 36
Schapira, Nathan, 93, 132
Scherman, Nosson, 51n22
Schochet, J. Immanuel, 19–20
Scholem, Gershon G., xvi, 9n17–18,
     54, 91n5, 110n13, 112–13,
     113n19
Schwartz, Howard, 21
Sebag, Yosef, 48n15, 100, 102n1,
     105n2, 3, 106n4, 5, 6, 7, 108n8
Sforno, Ovadiah ben Jacob, 33, 81
Shanks, Herschel, 5, 5n6
Sheinkin, David, 122n1
Shimon bar Yochai, 10, 28, 98n20
Shimshon of Ostropoli, 61–62, 62n46
Shlomo Yitzchak (Rashi), xv, 10, 24n3,
     29, 76, 80

Silberberg, Naftali, 111
Shneur Zalman of Lyady (Liadi),
     xiiin7, 75n26, 96n16
Sofer, Moses (Moshe Sofer or Moses
     Schreiber), 75, 76n15
Stamm, Johann Jakob, 6n1
Stern, Samuel Miklós, 85n31, 91n4
Strong, James, 118n24

Tanna D'Vei Eliyahu, 72
Theophory in the Bible, 138n1
Tishby, Isaiah, 92n7
Trachtenberg, Joshua, 109
Triester, Shmuel-Simcha, 98, 98n20
Trugman, Avraham Arieh, 109n9

Ulmer, Rivka, 5n3

Waskow, Arthur, 38, 131
Waton, Harry, xiv, 13n24, 94, 130
Wisnefsky, Moshe Yaakov, xiv, 13n24,
     42n5
Wolffsohn, David, 113, 115
Wolfson, Elliot R., 8, 58n39, 75n28

Yoreh, Tzemah, 38

Zakovitch, Yair, 37
Zobel, H.-J., 7n10
Zwickel, Wolfgang, 5, 5n6

Subject Index

Acrostic, 51, 63
Active (Agent) Intellect, 58–60, 88, 120
Anagram, 44–45, 96, 119–20
Ayin (Nothingness), 93

Bereshit ("In the beginning"), xii,
    xvi–xvii, xix, 17–18, 46n13,
    49, 51–55, 57, 66, 69, 72, 77,
    79, 82, 85, 102–3, 105–6, 117,
    122–23, 125

Death of the first-born, 61, 63

Earth (*Ha'aretz*), vii, xiii–xiv, 4–5,
    22–23, 46, 48, 71, 85, 95, 98,
    98n22, 104, 122, 125, 130, 133
Egypt, 4, 12, 27, 33, 49, 49n3, 56–57,
    62, 126, 130, 133
Ehyeh, 65, 120, 130
Eretz Yisrael (*Ysrael*), ix, 4, 21, 49, 69,
    78, 93, 132

Four Worlds, 18

Gematria, xiii, xv, 12–18, 20, 48n14,
    49–52, 54–55, 58–64, 66, 68–
    69, 75, 87–88, 93, 98–101,103–
    4, 108, 116–18, 120–21,
    124–27, 130

Heart, 52–55, 71–77, 79, 82, 84, 94,
    125, 133
Hevel, 118, 143

Hokhmah, xvii, 93, 100, 103–5, 108,
    120, 122–24, 132

K'lal Ysrael, 50, 119

L'cha Dodi, 51n29, 66, 85n31, 91n4,
    130
Letters of the alphabet, xiii–iv, xix,
    12–13, 52, 54, 88, 95, 101, 121
    Aleph (Alef), xiii, 14, 17, 45, 48, 55,
        66, 88, 93, 93n10, 105
    Bet (Beit), xiii, 14, 18, 51–55, 71–
        72, 77, 79, 88, 100, 121
    He (Hei), xiii, 14, 24, 48n16, 79, 100
    Lamed, 15, 17, 40–43, 45, 47, 51–
        55, 71–72, 77, 79, 93, 93n10,
        105, 121, 126
    Pe, 16–17, 52, 117, 121
    Resh, 16–18, 45, 93, 93n10, 105
    Sin, 16–18, 45, 104
    Vav, xiii, 14, 24, 40, 42, 48n16, 51,
        79, 103, 126
    Yod (Yud), 11–12, 15, 17–18, 24,
        41–43, 45–46, 48n16, 51,
        61n44, 63, 63n51, 66, 68, 76,
        79, 82, 100–101, 104, 121, 126

Makom ("Place"), 69
Mitzvah/Mitzvot, 51, 60, 68–69, 83,
    120, 130

Name (*Shem*), viii–xv, xviii, 3–7,
    20–28, 45–46, 119
Nefesh, xiv–xv, 58

Numbers,
  10 (ten), xii, xv, xvii, xix, 4–5,
      12, 18–20, 46–47, 50–52, 54,
      57, 60–63, 80, 87, 92–93, 99,
      101, 104, 110, 116, 120, 122,
      124–27, 129, 132
  28 (twenty-eight), 14–15, 80,
      102–3, 106, 122–124
  32 (thirty-two), xiii, xvi, 52–55, 121
  37 (thirty-seven), 106, 108, 118,
      123–24
  40 (forty), xvi, 15, 47, 62–64, 100,
      120, 132
  70 (seventy), xv–xvi, 12, 16, 48,
      56–58, 63, 68, 103, 133
  73 (seventy-three), 103, 105–6,
      108, 118, 123–24
  100 (one hundred), 16, 18, 67–68,
      101, 121
  186 (one hundred and eighty-six),
      16, 69
  231 (two hundred and thirty-one),
      xvii, 43, 87–88, 95–96, 99,
  430 (four hundred and thirty),
      16–18, 21, 100
  541 (five hundred and forty-one),
      xv–xvii, 17, 44, 58–69, 84, 88,
      93–94, 98–100, 102, 104, 108,
      116–17, 120–21, 123–25, 127,
      130, 132
  542 (five hundred and forty-two),
      17
  546 (five hundred and forty-six),
      17, 65, 98–100, 120, 127
  613 (six hundred and thirteen), 94,
      130, 130n1
  703 (seven hundred and three),
      xvii, 108
  913 (nine hundred and thirteen),
      103, 105–7
  1,081, 100–1, 121, 125
  2,701, xvii, 102–5, 108, 117–18,
      123, 127
  600,000, 46

Pardes (PaRDeS), xv, 6, 8, 10
  Derash, xv–xvi, 18–19
  Peshat, x, xv, 19, 25
  Remez, xv–xvi, 11–12, 19, 63
  Sod, xv, 9, 63, 89

Satan, 67, 75–76, 84, 120,
Shema, ix, 57, 84, 133
Shir ha-Shirim Zutta (*Haggadat Shir
      HaShirim*), 46, 142
Sof ma'aseh b'machshavah t'chilah, 85,
      125
Star Number, xvi, 116, 124
Star of David (Magen David), xvii,
      102–5, 108–117, 125, 127

Teeth (Tooth), 12, 52, 77, 121
Ten Commandments (Decalogue), 47,
      50, 63, 80, 122, 124
Ten Plagues, 47, 61–63
Ten Sayings (Utterances), xii, 46,
      46n13
Ten *Sefirot*, 19, 99–100, 110n13
Tetragrammaton (YHWH), 3, 11, 17–
      18, 20, 24, 40, 46, 48, 48n16,
      51, 53, 63, 65, 67–69, 71n2, 74,
      85, 94–95, 104, 110, 116–17,
      119–20, 124–27, 130
Tiferet, 19–20, 30n15, 93, 95, 100–101,
      120–21, 125, 132
Triangle (triangular) number or sum,
      101, 103, 107–9, 117, 121, 127

Vayishlach, xv, 21
Vowels, 12, 126

Wrestle, Wrestling match, 3, 21, 24–25,
      36, 38, 80–81, 83–85, 89, 131